Flying off the Shed Roof

Flying off the Shed Roof

Muriel Bridgewater

ATHENA PRESS
LONDON

Flying off the Shed Roof
Copyright © Muriel Bridgewater 2008

ISBN 978 1 84748 415 4

London Borough of Barnet	
Askews	Aug-2009
	£5.99

First published 2008 by
ATHENA PRESS
Queen's House, 2 Holly Road
Twickenham TW1 4EG
United Kingdom

Printed for Athena Press

Contents

Lamplighters, Pixie Hoods and Gracious Living

I was born in September 1942 into a house full of women. My arrival was the consequence of a three-day pass granted to my father, nine months earlier, from his war service with the RAF! For the first three years of my life I knew neither my father nor my uncles, and was entrusted to the tender care of my mother, my sister, my cousins and my aunts. We all tumbled happily and chaotically together in a gracious Edwardian house in Livingstone Road, Perry Barr – a once genteel suburb of Birmingham.

Livingstone Road was made up of large, double-fronted, three-storeyed Edwardian houses. During the 1940s most of the houses were still in private hands and not yet converted into nursing homes or bedsits. The houses had been designed to accommodate a large number of servants, who all had quarters in the attics. Butler's pantries, sculleries, flower rooms, coal cellars, tradesmen's entrances, bell pulls and so on were still very much in evidence as reminders of the work carried out behind the scenes in bygone days.

The road itself was gracious, too. It was clean and wide with very little through traffic. Householders swept and washed the pavements daily; litter and graffiti did not exist. The lamps that bordered the road were run on gas and were made of ornate cast iron with dazzling glass lanterns at the top. Inside the lanterns were the gas mantles and the levers used to turn the gas on and off. I imagine the present generation would find it hard to believe that the lamps were operated manually, night and morning, every single day of the year.

The lamplighter would arrive with a long pole, open the door and turn the levers. Of course his hours of work were much shorter in the summer when natural light could be relied upon! The lamplighter served another useful purpose. Many people used him as a 'knocker-up'. For a small reward he would regularly use his long pole to tap on the windows to wake the men for work. Perhaps alarm clocks were not generally available, or too expensive for working-class people to own.

I remember sitting in the holly-hedged front garden of Number 36 in my pushchair, dragging my feet in the dusty path, with the heavy scent of sweet alyssum drifting all around me, whilst I waited for my mother.

I always had to wear an 'itchy' pixie hood whenever we went for a walk. Pixie hoods were in fashion for girls and were easy and economical to knit. They consisted of two knitted squares of equal size, laid flat, one on top of the other, and sewn up along two sides. The ties were made from bits of crochet or ribbon. The wool for pixie hoods came from unravelled jumpers, which had worn through at the elbows. All wool seemed to be thick and scratchy and I hated my pixie hood. When I was a little older berets came into fashion and I loved them – they perched nicely on the top of your head and didn't itch anywhere.

Both the entrance to the house and the hallway were tiled with beautiful mosaic tiles in terracotta, blue and cream laid in an intricate geometric pattern. I thought the hallway was lovely, but Mom and Aunt Doll hated it because they had to get down on their hands and knees every week for many years to scrub it clean. I can actually see them kneeling, Cinderella-like, with an old galvanised bucket, floorcloth, bristly brush, and Vim in a rust-encrusted metal tin.

The staircase was elegantly carved and the treads were wide and deep. The carpet did not reach to the edge and was held in place by brass carpet rods with clips on either side. The ends of the clips were shaped like acorns. The banister was wide and highly polished ending in a huge newel post, the top of which was in the form of a large curled up snake. We slid down that banister often, coming to an abrupt halt at the bottom, astride the 'snake'.

Inside, to the right of the front door, was a well-proportioned room, complete with an ornate plaster ceiling, heavily panelled door, sash windows, and a grand marble fireplace, at the side of which was the servants' bell push. Mom used this 'drawing room' as her sitting room for entertaining visitors.

I have three vivid memories of events that took place in that room. Aunt Kath did not visit us often; the atmosphere was always tense due to a family 'falling-out'.

However, on one of her rare visits, my sister Linda and I were startled to see that Aunt Kath had bright red nail varnish on her fingernails – and her toenails! This was something we had never seen before and knew instinctively that our parents did not approve.

Aunt Kath was wearing rarely seen nylon stockings, and I can clearly recall the sound of her long fingernails scratching over her nylons to ease an itch on her leg. I ponder often over that little scene because I can still feel the undercurrent of disapproval shown to her on that occasion. I once asked my Uncle Fred why she was an outcast in the family and he said, 'I can't tell you, but she was a very naughty girl.'

The second memory is rather sad. I can remember being in the room with Mom and Linda when Dad came in. He leaned on the shelf above the fireplace with his head bowed and began to cry – an event that Linda and I had never witnessed before. There was a lot of quiet talk between him and Mom, and although Linda and I were worried and frightened they didn't explain to us that Grandma Rose had died in a perfectly natural manner and that Dad was crying for the loss of his mother. We didn't really understand what had happened until we moved into her empty house some months later.

The third memory makes me hoot with laughter. Aunt Doll and Mom were sitting at the dining table having a cup of tea and a good gossip. I can remember that I had been upstairs in the bathroom playing a game. I was about five or six.

The game involved walking along the edge of the enamelled bath and, of course, I slipped and fell astride the bath, seriously hurting myself in a very private place! I pulled my pants down and saw that I was bleeding. I ran downstairs to tell Mom, but before I had a chance to explain she saw the blood in my pants and more running down my legs. I shall never forget the look of absolute horror that passed between Mom and Aunt Doll. Their first instinctive thought was that, at six years of age, I had started my periods!

In the second ground floor sitting room, Aunt Doll kept her treadle sewing machine in front of the window to catch the best light. When she was not working at the machine, cousin Margaret and I used to take it in turns to sit on the chair and operate the treadle. It was a magical sensation to watch the many different sized wheels whirring round and round with the needle jumping up and down so fast you could hardly see it. Many times we muddled up the cotton, getting the bobbins into a terrible mess and the shuttles jammed. Aunt Doll used to come and sort it out in a rather tight-lipped way.

It was a very big room, and for many years Aunt Doll's entire family of five slept in it, and often I did too. It was not unusual in those days for a whole family to sleep in one room. In our case it was not lack of space, but just the economics of keeping rooms warm. There was coal enough for one bedroom fire, but not for two.

Aunt Doll's wardrobe was behind the door; it was like an Aladdin's cave. Aunt Doll never minded us dressing up in her clothes. She had many lovely fashionable outfits of the late forties and early fifties. Margaret and I spent hours parading up and down the hallway in her peep-toed high-heeled shoes, massive cartwheel hats, beads, long buttoned gloves, and princess-line dresses and coats. We wore her lipstick and rouged our cheeks and filled her handbags with grips, and powder compacts, and lace hankies, and combs, and old Woodbine packets. We could play 'dressing up' for days on end and never tire of it.

The last door on the right-hand side of the hallway led to the garden room. The most memorable thing about this room was the full width windows and doors made completely of stained and leaded glass. I was very young at the time but it made a lasting impression on me; I have only seen better examples in the most famous church windows.

At the end of the hall was the kitchen, used at this time by Aunt Doll as her living room. There was a fireplace, which I imagine had replaced the old blackleaded range. It was a typical 1930s rather ugly tiled fireplace with an open coal fire and back boiler.

At the side of the fireplace was a floor-to-ceiling cupboard, its use and purpose long since forgotten. Uncle Frank used it to store the buckets of nutty slack, wood kindling and newspapers needed to light the fires.

The kitchen, like several other rooms in the house had enormous sash windows. Sometimes the sashes would perish and break and the windows would come down with a crash. When the windows were working properly they could be opened to let the cooking steam escape from the adjacent scullery. The top window came down on the weights and dropped behind the lower one. There would then be a two-inch gap between the two frames. Many times silly little sparrows used to drop down from the roof above and fall between the two panes. It was nearly always impossible to get them out and I remember frantic efforts with sticks to free them.

The windows were a problem in another way. They had narrow inner windowsills just at toddler height and when we were standing looking out of the window we used to munch our teeth along the sills. The trouble was, at that time, all household paint contained lead so we had to be smacked for teething on the wood – lead poisoning was a serious threat in those days.

I remember, too, the blackout curtains. The kitchen window had black material on a roll at the top of the window with a cord dangling from it. At the end of the cord was a bobble to pull the curtain down when needed. The bobble was fastened round a hook on the windowsill. I can't explain how, as such small children, we realised that this routine of not showing a light during wartime was sacrosanct, but we did. Whatever other mischief we might get into, we never interfered with the blackout.

In one corner of the kitchen was the butler's pantry, very like those seen in period television dramas. Along the top of the wall, above the picture rail, there still remained the row of bells that summoned the maids and indicated where their services were required in the house.

Passing straight through the kitchen and down a steep step revealed the real workings of the house – the scullery! Aunt Doll used this as her kitchen; it housed a cooker, kitchen cabinets of sorts, an old stone sink with wooden draining board, an Ascot heater and a huge back door, which led down another step into a little covered area. On one side the area was open to the elements and often bitterly cold.

From the covered area there was another steep step down into the yard proper, where there were coal sheds, the wash mangle and an outside toilet, formerly an earth closet.

The side entry was the scene of one of my earliest rebellions. I suffered much at the hands of my older sister, Linda, when I was a toddler and rarely managed to get my own back on her for her constant taunting and teasing.

I don't recall what precipitated the final breaking of my patience but whatever it was I'd had enough. I ran on my fat little legs to the coal shed to fetch the axe and dashed off at full tilt after Linda wielding the axe in my hand. Linda ran screaming into the side entry with me, and the axe, close behind her. The entry was very long and narrow with a door halfway along leading up some steps into the hallway. Linda reached the doorway and ran in screaming loudly for Mom to rescue her – luckily she did, and Linda's head wasn't cleaved in two. The axe was no longer kept in the coal shed! It is an interesting trick of memory that Linda remembers this story the other way round: that is – she chased me.

Although much of the original statuary had perished, the gardens were still lovely, with borders and walkways surrounding a generous-sized central lawn. At the far end of the garden was a beautiful brick wall capped by the most enormously strong, curved dark blue bricks. Beyond this wall was a secret garden! We used to climb over the wall to wander in and out of the many trees, looking at the bluebells, daffodils and primroses, and playing all sorts of imaginative games.

We were chastised for doing this because it was actually the end of someone else's garden, but the grounds to their house were so vast that they never came down that far and never knew that we were there. The people who lived in the house were extremely wealthy; they had one little girl, who went away to school and was not allowed to mix with us. I'm sure she would have liked to.

On either side of the garden were ornate palings with arrow-head designs at the top. Most of these eventually disappeared, as people had to give them up to help the war effort. The palings were melted down and used to make armaments – or so we were told! For some reason, not all of the palings on the right-hand side of the garden were removed and those remaining were the cause of another accident.

Once again, Linda was the instigator of a dangerous game. I knew if I didn't join in I would be taunted with 'Cowardy, cowardy, custard – can't eat mustard!' as well as 'Mommy's little darling!' The game involved climbing up the compost heap at the bottom right-hand side of the garden to enable us to reach high enough to climb over the palings and from there into the house next door.

The neighbours on that side didn't like children and had none of their own; they saw us as a dreadful noise and nuisance. It was more challenging, therefore, for us to invade their garden. The idea was for me, as smallest, to go first so the others could give me a leg-up. I tried my best but, of course, at the last moment I slipped and fell and became caught on the palings. The arrowhead paling went straight through my arm in two places like a big darning needle.

I shudder now at the remembered pain and terror of being trapped on that paling whilst help was sought. I have a perfectly shaped arrowhead scar at the top of my right arm as a lasting memento of that day.

However, there are also many happy memories of playtimes with my sisters and cousins in the garden. There were bountiful fruit trees – pears, damsons and apples and we spent many summer days with the line props bashing the branches to make the fruit fall down. We munched our way through all of it, including grubs – we weren't selective and often had diarrhoea. You ate where and what you could when you were a war baby!

We all had bikes and scooters and ramshackle dolls' prams and spent hours and hours trundling around the long paths. We draped the clothes horse with blankets to make tents; we had rope swings and tree houses, and water fights in the summer. We had little patches of garden surrounded by stones to mark the plots. We grew lettuce and radishes and flowers such as pansies, lobelia and sweet alyssum ('Little Dorrit' – a name that I loved). I marvelled at the packets with the pretty pictures showing what was meant to happen with the seeds. The packets were threaded on sticks and stuck into the ground near to where the seeds were expected to grow. We sat patiently threading silver milk bottle tops on black thread, which was stretched across the plot to keep the birds off.

I was only three or four but already loved gardening. I can remember the feel of the hundreds of little seeds in my hand, and the worry of them slipping through my fingers. There seem such a few seeds in a packet now, but then I could hardly contain them all.

The radishes were best because they grew so fast. The trick was to plant just a few seeds on consecutive days to avoid a glut. Once they started growing we could go down to our plot every day and have the thrill of pulling up a few for a salad. Some were really round and fat and red, but others (pulled too soon) were long and thin and tasteless.

Whenever I recall my earliest gardening days and my amazement at how things grew I am reminded of giving my young son, Simon, a few rhubarb crowns to plant in his own bit of garden. He dug them up every single day for months to see if they were growing. In the end I begged a fully-grown clump from a friend and planted it at night for him to find next day. There was no hope of Simon's clumps ever growing into mature plants!

The room at the end of the first floor landing was our bedroom – just around the corner from Mom and Dad's room. I loved it because it was immediately above Aunt Doll's kitchen and I could hear the comforting buzz of conversation when I was in bed, and could often smell chips or bacon cooking for Uncle Frank's tea. That was not so pleasing, as we were always hungry.

The floor was covered with a square of lino surrounded by darkly stained floorboards. The floorboards did not fit very well in the corner nearest the window, and we discovered that if we crept out of bed and lay down on the floor with our eye to the corner, we could catch glimpses of what was going on downstairs. I don't think we ever saw or heard anything that we shouldn't but, even so, we thought we were hugely daring.

Usually there were at least two or three of us sleeping in that little room; we had our own small beds with the most wonderful blankets made out of knitted squares which had been sewn together. Nothing was wasted in those days, and even the tiniest lengths of wool were carefully kept and used to knit squares. I loved to lie in bed looking at the different colours. Some squares were all blue, or red or yellow or green, and others were multi-coloured where two strands of finer wool had been twisted together to give an even thickness. You could lie in bed for hours, pulling bits off the different squares and rolling the gathered fluff into soft multicoloured balls. Years later, my son Jonathan did the same thing when he lay in bed waiting for sleep to come. He stored the collected fluff safely in his ears!

The room was also used for quarantine, and then it was not such a happy place. In those days children were strictly isolated from one another when they had measles, whooping cough, chickenpox or mumps. I spent weeks alone when I had chickenpox, followed immediately by mumps. Mom and Aunt Doll would read to me when they could, but I wasn't allowed out of bed and none of my sisters or cousins were allowed in.

To add insult to injury Aunt Kath sent a Red Cross parcel with, amongst other things, chocolates in a really beautiful tin. I couldn't have any chocolates because my throat was swollen and I could only manage liquids for many days. I really expected Mom to save me some chocolate for when I was better but, amazingly, she didn't!

It is difficult to convey to people now what a devastating dis-appointment it was. We simply never had chocolate – it just didn't exist during those wartime days, and to receive some in a Red Cross parcel was like winning the lottery. I decided in my childish mind that I would settle for the beautiful box, but Mom gave it to Aunt Doll to keep her buttons in.

On the half landing was a long, low cupboard that was an indoor coalhouse! In the early 1900s the coal needed to heat the upper rooms of the house was brought up by servants and tipped into the cupboard. When we lived at Number 36 the cupboard was used for the same purpose. I can remember Mom struggling up the stairs with buckets of coal to tip into that cupboard.

I suppose it was preferable to making the long walk downstairs, along the hall, through the kitchen and scullery to the outside coal sheds when the weather might be wet and windy. I think life was hard for Mom, with three little children and the men away at war.

There was a large, empty room on this floor, too, that my cousin Margaret and I used to play in sometimes. One day we persuaded Margaret's brother, Roger, to set his trains out in there. He had a great deal of track, signals, sidings, level crossings, tunnels, bridges, points and stations, and two or three lovely engines with lots of coaches and goods wagons. We made a huge layout of it and it took us a very long time to get it all working properly.

We realised we were getting cold so decided to light a fire in the grate. We sneaked downstairs to collect anything burnable and came back with quite a haul, including matches. We soon had a really good fire burning, with flames leaping up the chimney at a terrific rate. After a very short time we heard an enormous roaring above our heads, together with a loud thumping down below at the front door.

Yes, we had set the chimney on fire and the flames were shooting out of the stack, seriously alarming the neighbours opposite. The fire brigade had to be summoned very quickly – not an easy matter when people did not have telephones!

The fire was eventually put out, but it had been extremely serious and strong enough to crack the bricks in the wall above the fireplace. The fire brigade charged ten shillings for their visit – a huge amount of money in 1950. For once there was no kindness meted out with our punishment; we were in serious trouble and we knew it.

Round the corner at the end of the first floor landing was a second flight of stairs to the top floor. This staircase, which was narrow, steep and uncarpeted, bore no resemblance to the grand staircase below.

The attic rooms initially housed a German couple and their small son. At the outbreak of war the German couple suffered dreadfully. The father of the family was interned for the duration of the war and the mother was cold-shouldered by everyone.

Mom and Aunty Doll tried to befriend her, but very quietly. You simply couldn't be seen as a German sympathiser then. I am ashamed to say that we treated their young son appallingly, regularly tying him up and playing games in which he was always a prisoner, always the enemy, and always bullied. We did get into trouble for this behaviour but we still played the games when we were unobserved. I sometimes worry about the psychological damage we may have caused that young boy.

After the war, the attic housed another childless couple who were extremely kind to us children and often gave us their sweetie ration. Linda would clamber up the stairs to Mrs Cartwright, knowing that she would be given two sweets – one for her and one for me. They were usually toffees wrapped in a twist of paper. Linda used to eat hers very quickly and then sit on the stairs sucking mine until it was nearly gone. Linda would then re-wrap it and leave it on the stairs for me to fetch. It was ages before I realised what was happening. Still, in those days, half a sweet was better than none!

At one time Mom lived in the small rooms at the very top of the house, which must have been very difficult with two babies to carry up and down. Linda and I were very young, both under two years of age, when a frightening thing happened. I don't remember the event but tales have been told about it many times. Mom checked that Linda and I were both safe and then made the long trek downstairs to hang out the washing on the line. When she came back she was absolutely petrified to see that a two-foot-long incendiary bomb had come straight down the chimney and was sitting in the hearth.

She grabbed Linda and me and ran back down the stairs, calling to everybody to get out of the house. The ARP warden was summoned and the bomb dealt with without any harm coming to anybody, but it could have been such a different story.

The cellar was a dark, damp basement that ran beneath the entire ground floor of the house. Access to the cellar was either through a door halfway along the inner hall, or up two steep stone steps that led off the tradesmen's long side entry. The door leading down to the cellar was kept locked because it was quite a dangerous place. A very steep flight of blue-black stone steps led down to a dungeon-like cavern. The steps were often damp and slippery and there was very limited light. On the back of the cellar door hung our row of gas masks, which we had to grab as we went down the cellar steps whenever there was an air raid.

At the far side of the cellar there was a mountain of coal and coke that had been dropped from above by the coal merchant. In the garden, near the front drawing room window, was a fancy ironwork grill decorated with a criss-cross, vine-leaf pattern. When the coalman came with his horse and cart, he would remove the grill, shout, 'Look out below!' and immediately tip several huge bags of coal down into the cellar, where it fell in a mountainous heap. If we happened to be down the cellar at the time we would be covered from head to foot in fine coal dust.

The light that filtered down from the grill was enchanting; on a sunny day the pattern on the grill made fascinating dancing movements on the walls that transformed their normal slimy green appearance.

Dad and Uncle Frank built themselves a good strong work-bench down there. They kept their many tools hanging on the wall above the bench and had stools to sit on whilst they worked. They had a big metal vice on the bench that was bought by Uncle Percy from Wolf's.

Dad and Uncle Frank made many of our toys at this workbench; there were certainly very few toys available in the shops and, even if there had been, there was no money to spare for them. They made beautiful wooden doll's house furniture, wooden and metal cars and trucks, bagatelle machines, building blocks, doll's cots and prams, scooters and bicycles, railway bridges, stations and sidings and much, much more.

There was a machine, too, in the cellar that gave us much enjoyment. It was rather like a treadle sewing machine, but instead of a needle going up and down there was a saw. Dad and Uncle Frank used it to make jigsaws. They collected the most wonderful coloured pictures from magazines, which they pasted onto plywood. When the pasted pictures were dry they were cut into intricately shaped pieces by the machine. As children, we had more jigsaw puzzles than anybody we knew, and spent many happy hours putting them together. We still do now!

When I remember the cellar I have very mixed feelings. It was a scary place, and whenever I see horror films with scenes set in cellars I can immediately identify with the terror portrayed. On the other hand, treasured toys and games were produced down there in the half-light; our fathers made them for us with love and care – and that's a good memory.

The house where I spent my infant years was a happy place; I think I had an idyllic start to life. I understand now, of course, that the country was at war and that we were shielded by virtue of our tender years. The house seemed to envelope us, to love us and to protect us, and I look back on my years within its walls with real affection.

Aunt Doll's Back Kitchen

The house we all shared in Livingstone Road had been divided into three flats. Aunt Doll, Uncle Frank and their children lived on the ground floor – and the heart of their home was the back kitchen. The kitchen was always warm and always smelled of cooking; it was forever full of people and cats, and filled with the sounds of music and laughter. It is not surprising that many of my childhood memories centre on it.

Life in the kitchen was lived at the coalface. Newspaper was spread on the table for a cloth; the usual lace doilies or starched tablecloths were nowhere to be seen because we could, and did, make a mess. So many memories of that kitchen remain. A row of defunct bells ran along the top of the wall with names beneath such as Dining Room, Drawing Room, Bedroom, Study. There were corresponding bell pushes in many of the rooms, and it was a great disappointment to us children that they no longer worked.

A brightly burning coal fire was constantly surrounded by a nursery fireguard, draped magnificently with the next week's clean clothes for Aunt Doll's family. Uncle Frank had a horror of wearing unaired clothes, and everything had to be pressed to a mirror to see if any trace of damp remained. On the shelf stood an electric clock, always twenty minutes fast. The same clock is still in use today some fifty years later – and it's still twenty minutes fast!

At the side of the fireplace was a built-in cupboard that was home to the coal, kindling and buckets of slack. Aunt Doll's cat, Snowy, adopted this cupboard as her nursery – the only place she would consider giving birth to her many litters of kittens. Snowy had sixty-two kittens during those years, and it was heavenly for us children to be surrounded by such lovely creatures. We have all grown up to be animal lovers, with a special affection for cats.

Food was rationed and our treats were few and far between; I can still remember the joy of sitting in Aunt Doll's kitchen eating a thick slice of bread liberally coated with lard and sprinkled generously with salt. I can also remember most vividly Aunt Doll making gravy in the meat tin, stirring Bisto round in a bit of fat at the bottom of the tin and adding cabbage water. Uncle Frank, or 'Faither' as he was called, was served first and sat in splendour at the table with its *Daily Mirror* covering.

Uncle Frank didn't like the idea of 'germs' and reckoned that tea towels were prime suspects as carriers! He was an inventive man and made a closed-in cupboard with a rail, which hung on the back of the scullery door. Trouble brewed for anyone who didn't put the towels away or left the cupboard door open.

Uncle Frank also made a special trolley to pull a very early cylinder vacuum around on long before they were designed to wheel or glide. Incidentally, Aunt Doll had been the model used in promotional leaflets for Hoover vacuum cleaners in the 1930s. She was a very glamorous lady.

The back kitchen always had an odd assortment of chairs: armchairs, dining chairs, children's chairs, folding chairs and high chairs. Their common feature was that they all had covers on to protect the original upholstery – and then to protect the covers they had more covers, and so on. Aunt Dolly still has covers on the covers on the covers…

The back kitchen and the scullery were greatly involved with washing of every kind: bodies, clothes, floors, windows, vegetables. We didn't care much for Monday washday. Our mothers were tired and cross, we got the scrag-mag leftovers of the Sunday joint for dinner, and we had to get to grips with the 'wringer' – a commonly used name for the mangle. Margaret and I would struggle to the yard with a heavy, two-handled galvanised tub full of water-laden sheets to deal with. Many a time we got the dripping wet sheets wrapped round and round the rollers and had to call for help.

As a memento of those days I acquired a lovely old mangle. I painted the cogs and ironwork brightly in red, green and black and restored the old wooden rollers, bringing them back to life with many coats of creosote. My grandchildren, Robert, James and Harriet, loved to turn the handle to watch the cogs, wheels and rollers going round and round. Even though I put wet tea towels between the rollers to show them how it worked, they can't quite believe that washing was done in such a manner when I was a child. Six-month-old Joe has to wait a little while before he too can experience the pleasure of working the mangle!

I remember with horror the nastiness of the nappies being washed. Most dirt was either shaken or scraped off with a stick into the outside 'lav'. The terry towelling nappies were then sluiced up and down in the kitchen sink before being placed on the stove in a big saucepan of boiling water. They were poked at regular intervals with a wooden stick worn thin in the middle. Eventually they were rinsed three times in the sink – a blue bag being added to the last rinse to give them a good colour. Nappy washing was a daily chore.

The week's veggies were prepared in the very same sink; a good scrubbing down with a bristly brush and Vim was all that was required between nappy washing and food preparation.

Washing off the daily grime also took place in the sink; Uncle Frank washed and shaved in it, small children were bathed in it, hair was washed and deloused in it. The upstairs bathroom – the only one between the three flats – was used by prior mutual agreement and consent.

There was much argy-bargy about who was due to clean the bathroom and who cleaned it last. Toilet paper was non-existent – neat newspaper squares hung on a loop of string by the door.

Sunday was a big day for the washing of bodies and hair. Clean clothes from around the fireguard were removed and put out ready for Monday morning. At least this was so for Aunt Doll's family. I have no recollection of where my clean clothes came from, or how my mother managed in her upstairs flat. I only know that we were always clean, clothed and fed.

Aunt Doll was often into moneymaking schemes, and the back kitchen figured very large in these ventures. One Christmas she took in outwork from a local company; the job was to make up and box Christmas baubles. The kit consisted of bags of very delicate silver balls, looped bits of wire and strips and squares of cardboard which had to be made into boxes. Each box was to contain six completed baubles, and for each perfect box she would receive 6d.

Aunt Doll saw pound signs before her eyes and gathered us children round the kitchen table to set up her production line. She hadn't accounted for our clumsy little fingers or the amount of breakages four small children could achieve in half an hour. We thoroughly enjoyed it but the scheme was soon abandoned.

The football pools and backing the gee-gees was a major pre-occupation for Aunt Doll. She loved having a gamble and was often quite lucky. In those days gambling was illegal and there were no betting shops. Tallymen used to stand on street corners taking illegal bets from local people. After lots of discussion and scanning of the *Mirror*, a horse was picked, and with great whispering and secrecy a sixpenny piece was wrapped in a piece of paper with the bet written on it. One or two of us children would be sent off with the tiny package with strict instructions to speak to no one but the tallyman. We didn't really know what we were doing, but found it very exciting because we usually got a halfpenny to spend at the local sweet shop on the way home. I have no recollection of how winnings were paid – perhaps the tallyman brought them round after dark.

That back kitchen brought the world to life – Aunt Doll and Uncle Frank believed life was for living and to enjoy. They were the only people I knew in my childhood who had a radiogram and later on a television set. Were Mom and Dad poor, or did they think themselves too genteel for these diversions? All I can remember in our own flat was a very crackly radio for adult use only.

The radiogram was wonderful. Uncle Frank had a big collection of records, particularly Joseph Locke and Mantovani, and when we could get needles we had lovely times listening to the music.

Margaret and I used to tie our dressing gowns round our waists like ball-gowns and dance away whilst Aunt Doll and Uncle Frank sang 'Violetta' and 'I'll Take You Home Again, Kathleen'.

The television was bought and installed in the back kitchen in time for the Queen's Coronation in 1953. We knew of no other house in the vicinity with a television at that time. Hordes of us sat spellbound in front of a tiny 9" black and white screen, never thinking for one moment that anything more wonderful would ever be invented. Later on Uncle Frank bought a huge, thick magnifying glass on a stand, which stood in front of the television to make the picture bigger!

The kitchen was also home to Uncle Bill (Frank's brother). He was seriously diabetic, and came every day to have something to eat and to do his insulin injection. As children we got so used to seeing him tightening a band round a bulging arm or leg and sticking a needle in that we thought nothing of it – it was part of everyday life to us. None of us grew up to be fearful of injections – perhaps that was why.

Uncle Bill drove a taxi – a really magnificent vehicle with four doors, white covers on the seats and flowers on the back ledge. It had beautiful chrome fittings and a lovely walnut veneer dashboard. Often on a Sunday evening he would take Aunt Doll and her family to a pub for a drink, and often I was included. I used to love to go. I felt so grown-up. Once again, this was something Mom and Dad frowned upon and would never do – Dad thought drinking and pubs were sinful. In adult life I discovered that my paternal Grandfather had been a drinker, which perhaps had caused unhappiness for my father.

Uncle Frank was a great tease and I used to worry all the way to the pub because he would say to me, 'Have you got any money to buy us a drink?' Of course I never had any money and the outing was a bit spoiled because I didn't understand the joke no matter how many times he used it. We used to go to the pub called The Malt Shovel.

My cousins, Margaret and Roger, and my sister Linda, and I spent many of our earliest years together in the back kitchen of the house in Livingstone Road. All the memories are happy; I can feel and smell the atmosphere of it all to this day. In a way I grieve for the lost communal way of living we experienced. We were shared children with shared mums and we never lacked a hug, a kiss – or a scolding.

Grandad's Garden

My maternal grandparents, Charlie and Fanny Ross, were 'in trade', owning greengrocery and fishmonger shops in the area of Victoria, Whitehead and Albert Road in Aston. Grandad ran the shops, with the help of his daughters, alongside working as a carpenter; a trade with which he was associated for more than fifty years. I don't remember the shops, as my grandparents moved to Lichfield from their home in Crompton Avenue, Handsworth, when I was three years old.

The cottage in Lichfield was small and pretty, situated on the Birmingham Road at the top of Shortbutts Lane, where another branch of the family lived. It was truly a lane then with just a few houses and a village shop, but now it has speed bumps and traffic calming measures.

Grandad was a terrifying person. We were all scared of him: he was the epitome of a stern Victorian gentleman. His word was law. He had two favourite tricks with which to frighten us. The first, only mildly scary, was to bend down pretending to kiss us when, with a sudden swoop, he would grab us and rub his really sharp stubby beard over our soft-skinned faces. We hated it but didn't dare run away, and Mom, then in her thirties, was still too fearful of him to protect us.

The second trick was much more terrifying. During his time working in the fishmonger's, Grandad had lost the ends of several fingers on both hands due to gutting fish. Fish bones had become lodged under his skin, causing infection, and he had amputations of either one or two sections of fingers on both hands. His pleasure was to come right up close to us, lift his grotesque hands and stub the remaining bits of fingers into our faces, laughing his head off all the while. Mom never reproached him; I know she really felt for us but was too nervous of him to stop it.

Grandad was a referee for the Birmingham League for many years and had rows of pictures pasted to the scullery wall of teams he had been involved with (including Aston Villa). I am sure he treated the teams with the same strictness he showed his family. He was also a militant union man and had his name in the local paper more than once for his outspoken views.

Any feeling of affection I had for Grandad surfaced when he took me into his garden. It was the most wonderful place. There was no lawn or formal part of the garden – it was a typical working country garden but oh, the thrill of walking down the long path looking at row upon row of fruit and vegetables! Grandad grew everything you could possibly imagine: beans, peas, parsnips, carrots, onions, potatoes, cabbage, sprouts, beetroot, lettuce, radishes and every kind of fruit, all in their own season.

In amongst the rows of vegetables he grew marigolds to keep the pests down, and I still grow marigolds myself today for the same reason.

There were small square plots built up with odd bricks, filled with compost and surmounted by majestic marrows and cucumbers.

In the greenhouse there were rows and rows of bright red tomatoes, which we shook gently to pollinate. In the greenhouse, too, were huge bunches of grapes. The gnarled old root of the vine was outside the greenhouse and the fruit hung in clusters inside; this fascinated me as a child.

I can still remember the almost overwhelming smell of a long row of sweet peas grown for the house. The colours were jewel-like, with the flowers growing up long sticks made out of neatened up twigs from the trees. The sweet peas had to be picked every day to encourage new growth, so visitors were easily persuaded to take a bunch home.

All Grandad's love and tenderness went into that garden – he seemed, to me, to have none left over for anything else. He was forever confused in my mind with Mr McGregor in Beatrix Potter's *Peter Rabbit* stories… I wonder if she knew him?

Grandma, on the other hand, was lovely – exactly like a storybook grandmother. She had the most beautiful white hair, worn long and tied back with a bow at the nape of her neck with soft, fluffy wisps around her face. Her face was wrinkled and rosy like an old Cox's apple, always smiling and patient. Gran was always at home in a well-worn, flower-patterned dress covered by a snowy apron – busy with her endless chores.

The cottage was small but not easy to keep. There were home-made rag rugs on the stone floors. The floors had to be washed constantly, as the front door led straight off the street into the living room. This room held me spellbound as a child. In one corner stood a door behind which was a steep, narrow staircase leading to two bedrooms – I don't recall ever going up there. There was no bathroom. The toilet was an earth closet outside; it consisted of a hard, wooden bench seat with a dark, deep trench beneath it. I used to worry about falling down the hole.

There were several other enthralling things in that small room. The favourite was 'the glass ship'. It had pride of place on the sideboard and had been brought home by Grandma's father, who had been employed on a shipping line running some of the first Cook's holiday tours. It is said that he and his passengers were lost at sea on a subsequent cruise.

The ship was made completely of glass: the sails, the rigging, the crew, the waves, the lighthouse – everything – and all enclosed in a magnificent glass dome. Curiosities such as this (known as friggers) were popular in the late nineteenth and early twentieth centuries. Glassmakers made them in their spare time to relieve the humdrum work of producing everyday items over and over again. Sailing ships were the most popular and certainly demonstrated the glassmaker's skills.

Nearly as popular was a huge brassbound trunk, which stored the clothes of Grandma's relatives, long since dead. If we were very good Grandma would let us look at the clothes. There were beautiful floor-length dresses with beads, bustles, embroidery and satin bows, together with soft leather boots with dozens of little buttons. There were hats too, with lace frills, feathers and ribbons and gloves of every kind. I often wonder what happened to them all.

And finally, out of reach of our clumsy inquisitive fingers, but thrilling when we were picked up to look, was a cabinet full of the most wonderful knick-knacks collected over many years.

Grandma loved small things, and most were only one or two

inches high; little men on horseback, small teapots, cruets and jugs, posy vases and miniature men and women in fancy clothes, keepsakes of every kind. These are now dispersed around the family amongst Grandma's many grandchildren.

In the cottage there was a small kitchen and scullery without the benefit of any modern conveniences. Gran had brought up her big family of six children without the help of washing machines, fridges or vacuum cleaners. The kitchen always smelled delicious, as Gran was forever bottling produce from the garden. I loved looking at the jars high up on the shelf. They were called Kilner jars, specially made for the purpose of preserving food.

Gran's jars contained everything – damsons, plums, pears, pickled onions, beetroot, walnuts, and every kind of jam and marmalade. I especially loved the damson jam; the stones were always left in and, with a warning not to swallow them, we were given big slices of bread and jam to eat. I liked to see how long I could suck the stones before the taste disappeared. Sometimes a stone split and there was a little nut inside.

Gran also made parsnip wine. I can remember the lovely golden colour of the wine in long, slim-necked bottles with cork stoppers. I believe it was extremely potent – I have heard many stories about its strength around the family.

I don't remember Grandad dying at all. But Gran was different; I still feel sad about it now. In her eighties she was well looked after by her many daughters, but she still died alone, maintaining her independence to the end. Dad and my younger sister Lorna found her, on the morning of her death, lying across the cooker; I like to think she had been warming a little milk for her breakfast.

The cottage in Lichfield has changed beyond recognition. The pretty Hansel and Gretel house of my memory has been thoroughly modernised and upgraded. To me it now appears characterless and without the charm it once had.

I prefer not to look too closely when I drive past these days. Instead I let the memories of my gentle Grandma come flooding back, remembering her as she stood at the gate with a bunch of sweet peas in one hand and a tea towel in the other.

Congregational and Beyond

Tradition and ritual were the order of the day on Sundays when I was growing up. Everything that happened on Sunday was different and set apart from the other days of the week. For instance, breakfast might take a little longer if we had something cooked rather than cereal and the house seemed chaotic as Mom tried to oversee the slightly more elaborate breakfast as well as thinking ahead to Sunday dinner. She also had to organise four sets of clean clothes for Sunday school.

We always went to Sunday school in the morning to the Congregationalist Church at the top of Livingstone Road. Congregational Churches were individual churches, largely self-governing, which merged with the United Reformed Church in 1972. Sadly, our church has been demolished, apart from one fragmented section. According to a handmade sign hanging from its walls, this relic now houses a Caribbean bakery. It looks quite incongruous, as there is still a very pretty round stained glass window in one wall – the only reminder that it was once a church.

Mom never had our clean clothes ready; they were usually washed but never completely dried and certainly not aired. The socks were the worst problem – we only had one pair of white socks each, and they simply had to be clean for Sunday. If we had worn them on Saturday, Mom used to scrub them on the wooden draining board with a nailbrush and green soap in an effort to get them clean and dry for Sunday. Of course they never did dry, as we had no central heating and only a small coal fire in the living room. To avoid going out in wet socks Mom used to put them under the grill and then, as she did when toasting bread, promptly forgot all about them. Many, many times we went to Sunday school with brown scorch marks on our socks running crazily from knee to ankle!

Our Sunday school teacher was called Miss Lamb, and she

really was meek and mild and gentle. We believed deeply and sincerely in Jesus and everything we were told from the Bible. I remember that we worried about doing anything wrong, telling lies or misbehaving, because we knew with a sure certainty that Jesus was watching us. In Sunday school we coloured in religious pictures, learned and sang hymns and were told stories from the Bible.

As we got older we spent less and less time in the Sunday school class and more and more in church proper. I don't know that any of us were particularly devout, but we knew that being part of the congregation would eventually lead to being members of the youth club, and that was a very desirable thing. Social life in those days definitely revolved around the church.

Once a year the whole church would join together to practise for the 'Anniversary'. To be honest I don't know what it was the anniversary of, but it was an important celebration in all churches in my youth and looked forward to, and worked towards, for many months. For the anniversary, all generations of the church joined together to learn hymns and anthems that would be performed twice on Anniversary Sunday, once in the morning and once in the evening.

Our choirmaster, Mr Barlow, was very good at training everyone to give a polished performance. It amused us greatly because our Sunday school teacher, Miss Lamb, married Mr B*aaaar*low. They had to endure a lot of teasing from us all as we deliberately mispronounced his name to imitate a sheep bleating.

As well as the hours and hours of practising to make sure we were word-perfect and could hit the right notes, everyone had to be kitted out with an anniversary outfit – new dresses for the girls, and shirts and ties for the boys. It was the only time we ever had a new dress and so it was looked forward to with great anticipation. When we were small Mom used to scrape together odd pennies until she had enough to take us to a dressmaker called Mrs Farmer, who lived in Lozells. She made us lovely dresses for many years, and I do remember well the thrill of being allowed to put my new dress on for the anniversary; we had new socks and ribbons, too. No scorch marks on this special day! When Linda was old enough she made our anniversary dresses. She was a very talented seamstress and, when she reached her teens, could literally make a dress on one evening to wear the next.

For the anniversary, several young men from the church worked for many hours building a tiered stage at the front of the church. The planks used were covered in cloth and we either stood or sat on them, according to our height, to give the right effect. Today's sophisticated children probably cannot imagine how much we enjoyed the day, but the atmosphere in the church was electric. We looked down from our platform and every pew was full of people waiting to hear us sing – and sing we did, with all our hearts. The swell of the music and song in the church was superb and the soloists were spectacular. Both as a small child and as a teenager, tears pricked my eyes with the emotion of it all.

After the evening performance there was a supper provided for all those who had taken part, as well as for the congregation who had come to watch and listen; but normally after Sunday school we would go home to Sunday dinner. This was sacrosanct in those days after the shortages of war and because families were reunited for the first time in many years, with fathers sitting at their own tables once again.

In our house we always had a leg of lamb or a joint of beef for Sunday dinner, together with roast potatoes, mashed potatoes (except for me because I hated them), peas, cabbage or sprouts. We always had mint sauce made with a few sprigs of mint from the garden; they were sprinkled with sugar and chopped on a board until fine enough to put into an eggcup with a drop of vinegar.

With the beef we had mustard, which was made by mixing a dry, bright yellow powder with water. It was always either too runny or too thick and turned the spoon bright green if it was left in the pot for too long. We always had a pudding on Sunday. This was usually apple or treacle tart with custard, or rice pudding. Dad loved the skin on rice pudding, so we rarely got to taste it. The skin was dark brown and wrinkly, generously sprinkled with nutmeg. The pies were made using home-made pastry in a flat white enamelled dish with a blue rim. A white china funnel in the shape of a blackbird supported the pastry lid. The steam escaped through the blackbird's open mouth. When the pie was cut I can remember the scraping noise the knife made on the dish. I am sure we all got a portion of the enamel in with our pie. The plate was certainly very scored.

The custard was made in an old cracked basin, which lived on the cold slab in the pantry. I am sure it was the same basin in which Mom mixed her hair dye! The custard was lovely, though. Once again, it was Dad's privilege to have the skin.

Our social life revolved around the church, and we were all staunch members of the youth club, as well as belonging to the Brownies and later, the Guides. Every now and again the youth club used to put on a play to raise funds for the church. I was never in any of the plays because I always felt too shy to take part, but Linda had parts in several. In *Jack and the Beanstalk* Linda took the part of Jack's mother. In one scene Jack's mother was wringing her hands and talking to Jack about their lack of money. Linda brought the house down by coming to the front of the stage, putting her hands on her hips, bending forward confidentially to the audience and saying, 'We got no money for the mortgage on the cow.' In another play, the title of which I cannot remember, she and three friends had to get dressed up like dogs' dinners for a planned outing. With great disappointment they received a message from stage off that the outing was cancelled. Again Linda caused much laughter by coming forward to the centre of the stage and telling the audience in a most exaggerated way, 'We're all dressed up and nowhere to go!'

We also had beetle drives in the church hall and these were great fun. I cannot remember the exact rules but, basically, tables were set out around the hall, with four people sitting at each. You were given a piece of paper and a pencil and on the shake of the dice you could begin drawing your beetle. Perhaps it was six for a body, and five for a head, three for legs, and so on. When you had finished your first beetle you moved to the next table and then the next. The first to complete the circle of tables was the winner.

After youth club, theatre, beetle drives, Brownies, Guides or Evening Church we all hung around outside chatting and flirting. It was the way you met boys in a fairly safe environment, and many of the older boys and girls went on to start walking out together (courting), getting engaged and then married.

It was during one of these get-togethers outside the church one Sunday evening that I encountered the very first black person I had ever seen. I stared and stared at this little girl very hard; I really did think there was something dreadfully wrong with her and I felt pity for her. One or two of the crowd went up to her and touched her skin and felt her woolly hair that was fastened by white satin bows into two stiff plaits.

We must have frightened that little girl, but we genuinely didn't understand. None of us had ever seen a West Indian before. As time went on, a few more of that race appeared and joined the church; they looked fabulous on Sundays, the women wearing very colourful clothes and lovely hats, the children immaculate with bows in their hair and party dresses. All the men wore smart suits and trilby hats; their shirts gleaming brilliantly white against their black shiny skin. As children we were very curious about our new neighbours but, like children everywhere, accepted them into our midst without question.

It seemed so much simpler when I was a child. We needed the skills of people from other continents because so many of our workforce had been lost at war. The Government led a huge campaign in Africa and the Caribbean encouraging folk to come to Britain to work and we willingly held out our hands of friendship and welcome.

We had all read and loved the stories about black children in *Milly-Molly-Mandy*, *Uncle Tom's Cabin* and *Topsy*. When I read such stories I longed to meet the children and felt very fond of them. I think these books are probably frowned upon in school today.

The Brownie Pack and Guide Pack attached to the church also played a very big part in our lives. We attended evening parades, church parades, and summer camps for many years. We learned about belonging to a community, about teamwork, about having pride in what we did, and how to look smart. We were taught about keeping our uniforms immaculate, how to polish our shoes and our leather belts, to brush our berets, to Brasso our Brownie and Guide badges, to brush our hair until it shone, to darn our socks, and to make elastic garters to hold them up.

We learned to iron and fold the kerchief that went around our neck, to make a really good cup of tea, to tie reef knots, light a campfire with one match, to recognise the flags of many countries, and to send messages with flags using a signalling method called semaphore. We learned to cook and to sew, to knit and to blanket stitch, we learned first aid, to re-roll bandages and to make slings for broken arms.

We learned to sterilise needles for removing splinters, to dig deep holes for latrines, to pitch a tent, to roll sleeping bags and to set up a camp kitchen. Each time we achieved a task to the satisfaction of our guide leader (Brown Owl), we were given a small embroidered badge to stitch on the sleeve of our uniform. Many of us had badges in double rows from our shoulders to our wrists because we loved learning the tasks, and it was a joy to take part.

When annual Brownie and Guide camps came around we were usually lucky enough to attend. However, I let the side down on the first camp I went to. I wasn't very old and it was my first time away from home. I shouldn't really have gone because I had a very bad injury to my knee at the time caused, as usual, by Linda. She had dared me to jump off a moving bus and I fell badly in some rough gravel, getting stones embedded deep under my skin. My knee went septic and I had red-hot poultices put on it for many weeks to draw the stones out. The poultice was made by putting a tin of thick grey ointment (kaolin) supplied by the doctor in a saucepan of boiling water until it was very hot. Dad used to smear a dollop of the hot ointment on to a piece of lint and slap it quickly onto my knee whilst I shrieked my head off.

The treatment was still in progress when I went off to camp, and it fell to Tawny Owl to continue with it. This, together with being bitten to death by hundreds and hundreds of midges every night, caused me great distress, and I cried and cried to go home. Eventually someone had to walk the several miles to a telephone box to get a message through for Dad to fetch me home. I don't actually know how this was achieved because we didn't have a telephone at home, but I was fetched home before the end of the camp.

Another memory of camp is of Mom sitting up all night to get a navy cardigan finished for Linda to take with her. We went to bed the night before camp with all our kit packed and ready to go. Linda was really worried about not having her cardigan to complete her uniform, so Mom said she wouldn't go to bed until she had finished it. When we got up next morning poor Mom was still sitting in the armchair knitting with her eyes nearly shut. She just could not finish the cardigan in time and we had to leave without it. Unknown to us, she still carried on knitting after she had waved us goodbye. As soon as the knitting was finished and the cardigan sewn up, Mom wrapped it up into a brown paper parcel, tied it with string and took it to the post office. She posted it to the farmer in whose field we were camping, and asked him to give it to Linda as quickly as possible in case she was cold.

On another camp, I was on cookhouse duties with a couple of guides. We were making French fry for breakfast. This was made by dipping slices of bread into beaten egg, then frying the coated bread gently on both sides.

Because there were so many of us we had to beat together about thirty eggs – that was my job. I started cracking the eggs into a big basin and when I got to the last egg, I cracked it into the basin with a flourish and, to my horror, saw that the final egg was completely black and mouldy and smelled very bad. Before anybody could see that I had ruined thirty eggs, I quickly scooped out as much as I could and swiftly mixed in the rest. As I never ate eggs I wasn't that bothered and just kept my fingers crossed that no one would notice. I cooked the French fry a little more than necessary to hide the taste; there were no comments, so I think I got away with it!

As we grew older, our association with the church lessened and lessened. We began to find that we had outgrown the youth club and we were now too old for Guides. We could have joined the Rangers, but for some reason did not. Perhaps, having belonged to both Guides and Brownies from the age of seven through to fifteen, we had had enough of uniformity, regulation and honour and we wanted to rebel a little.

I don't know when it first started, or how our parents allowed it, but all of my peer group, as well as my sisters and cousins, got involved with rather a strange 'club'. Today it might be called a fringe religion or even a brainwashing sect.

The man who 'recruited' us was called Mr Keatley, and he seemed quite a wealthy man. He lived in a large house in Handsworth called The Gables, with a small church-like building at the end of the garden. We used to go very regularly to his house and into the 'church' where he preached to us.

He made us feel very welcome and encouraged our attendance with treats that were not normally available to us. For instance, we had no access to popular music, so he would make sure that whilst we were there he played records for us by Johnnie Ray and Frankie Laine – the pop stars of the early fifties. Of course, we loved it and always wanted to go back for more.

Mr Keatley's niece was a well-known cinema star called Violet Pretty, and we loved to get first-hand information from him about the stars and Hollywood. The cinema was important to us, as we had no television.

In reality I don't think Mr Keatley influenced our lives in any important way. I do still like to hear Johnnie Ray and Frankie Laine on the radio and be taken back to those times by their music, and I do like to remember how we dressed up and tried to look our best for our visits to The Gables. I really think it was more to do with the opposite sex though than with Mr Keatley's preaching – and he never did us any real harm.

He was more likely just one of the world's genuinely good people endeavouring to persuade youngsters to take the right path through life.

And so we grew up; we transferred seamlessly from Sunday school to Youth Church and to Fellowship, and from Brownies to Guides to youth club and beyond. Our course was safe and sure and predictable. We went from festival to festival, from routine to routine, from season to season and from year to year, in a never changing rhythm. Our pleasures were simple, and our life seemed undemanding and the sun shone every day.

War and Peace

I was three years old by the time the war finished, and I have some very vivid memories of the ways in which it affected my world. Of course, rationing and shortages continued for many years after the war, and I was about eight years old before all goods could be bought freely without coupons.

There are very many memories about food – or more precisely the lack of it. Everything was rationed, and each person was issued with a ration book that had to be used for all purchases of food, drink and clothing. The allocation of sugar, tea, margarine, meat, fish – everything – was worked out to the last ounce. The shopkeeper cut the coupons out of the book in exchange for goods, and that was it for the rest of the week. You could not go back to the shop for more if you ran out. No food could be purchased without the appropriate coupon to cover it.

The Ministry of Food had worked out the amount of food that the civilian population could survive on but, as the war dragged on, there was less and less available. Of course, there were no imports during wartime, so women were called upon to work on the land in an effort to provide enough basic vegetables for the home population. The mobilised women were known as the Land Army.

We had a spoonful of welfare orange juice and cod liver oil each day to supplement our very meagre diet, as well as to prevent the onset of rickets and scurvy. Most children hated the cod liver oil, but it was essential to take it and we were forced to do so. The orange juice and a sweet, sticky malt extract called Virol were much more acceptable.

When potatoes and eggs ran out, which they very often did, we had to use tins of dried potato powder (Pomme) and tins of dried egg. The Pomme was truly disgusting and I hated it. Mom must have been so distressed trying to feed three toddlers on this never varying, dismal, tasteless diet.

Mom used to mix the Pomme with water and put it on a plate, where it ran about like thick white soup. To liven it up and make it a bit more appetising, she would pour over bacon grease drained from our weekly rasher and slice up one tomato to garnish the top. It was truly hideous, but starvation made us eat it. I heave now if anyone serves me very creamy mashed potato. Incidentally, I don't remember where the actual rasher of bacon went – we only got to taste the fat that dripped from it during cooking.

An enduring memory, too, is that of sitting in my pram and waiting, waiting, waiting in long queues outside every shop in Perry Barr. Rumours went round all the time that so and so shop had, say, bananas or a little bit of meat.

Everyone rushed to get in line with their ration books in the hope that they would get to the front of the queue before the supply had run out. There was often disappointment, and we would trudge home again empty-handed.

Sweets and chocolate were unheard of. They were not thought a necessary foodstuff and so were not available. There were tickets in the ration books for confectionary, but in very miniscule amounts. Sweets were, in fact, one of the very last items to come off rationing in about 1952, I think. As children we longed for something sweet. Mom once very daringly used a small part of our minute margarine ration, together with a tiny bit of sugar, to make Linda and me some sweets. She cut the margarine into very small squares, rolled them in a bit of sugar and gave us a few each to suck. It was heaven, but we had to have dry bread for the rest of that week because we had used our margarine ration, and jam was non-existent.

Another of Mom's recipes was made with semolina. This is hard to describe; semolina is fine ground rice, which is mixed with milk and heated in a saucepan until it thickens. Really it tastes like nothing on earth. I suppose it looks like thick, white custard, but with a much more granular texture. Mom used to pile it up in our dishes, and to sweeten it would put on one or two blackberries that she had picked locally. When we squashed the blackberries into the peaked-up semolina it looked like blood, so Linda and I used to call the pudding 'Murder on the Alps'. The only way we could stomach this horrid mess was by making a game of it.

Linda got into the most awful trouble once because she found Mom's ration book in its hiding place, cut out a sweet coupon, hid it in her knickers pocket, went to the shop, chose the sweets, and ate the whole family's ration for that week on the way back home. This was an unimaginable crime in those days, but you can understand the temptation because we went without so much, and at times it got to be more than you could bear.

Our family was luckier than most, because Aunt Kath was in the Red Cross and she would send us the occasional food parcel. The excitement when these rare parcels arrived was almost enough to kill us. The food was contained in stiff, brown, square, cardboard boxes with a red cross stencilled on the top. Inside the box there was often a very small bar of chocolate, strips of mint-flavoured chewing gum and a packet of very waxy cheese slices, bright yellow in colour.

There were other items that I cannot remember; they held no importance for me. It was the cheese, chewing gum and chocolate that we loved the best, and Mom made these treats last for as long as possible.

When things were going very badly in the Midlands and the bombs were falling thick and fast, Mom decided that we should be evacuated to Wales, as were many children from cities such as Birmingham and Coventry.

Mom couldn't bear the thought of sending me and Linda to strangers, so she decided to try to find lodgings in Wales for the three of us. Luckily, she obtained a billet with a lady in South Wales in a village called Llantwit Major. I don't remember the village, but that is probably because we were not there for very long. Linda was a little devil, apparently, so Mom had to pack up and bring us home.

Firstly, Linda stole a jar of jam out of the landlady's pantry, together with two spoons. She carried the jar upstairs and we sat together in my cot, one at each end, chanting, 'A spoon for you and a spoon for me,' until all the jam was gone. Secondly, Linda's acute boredom in bed one morning encouraged her to strip off the wallpaper as far as she could reach. Poor Mom had to make good the cost of redecorating the room, as well as replacing the jam, and we were all packed off home to Birmingham to take our chances with the Germans!

We knew the Germans were our enemy but obviously didn't understand anything about the war. We did know that when the air raid sirens sounded all kinds of havoc began. We were pushed and pulled and hurried about, shouted at and smacked if we didn't instantly finish our game and get down the cellar. The cellar was vile; it was dark and dank and dirty and very, very frightening. Mom had to grab our gas masks on the way down and hang them around our necks. It was an offence, punishable by a fine, to go anywhere without your gas mask at any time, never mind when there was an air raid on.

I hated my gas mask. It was made of black rubber with a tube like an elephant's trunk coming from it, through which you were supposed to breathe if there was a germ attack. Fortunately this never happened, but we had to have regular practices with our masks. I reckon panic attacks and claustrophobia in my generation could well have started because of the conditions we had to endure during air raids. As soon as the sirens sounded we knew that there were hours of misery ahead. I hated and dreaded the sound of them. Sometimes today I hear factory sirens that sound a bit similar and it gives me the creeps.

Clothes too were on ration, and coupons were needed to buy anything new to wear. There was great excitement once because someone had got hold of an old parachute that had gone beyond repair. Parachutes were made of fabulous silk, and when they were unpicked and re-sewn a whole neighbourhood of women could get a pair of knickers, a blouse or an underskirt from one parachute. The parachute cords, too, could be unravelled, as they were made up of many strands of silk thread. When all the plaited strands had been undone, we used to roll the silk thread into balls that were put away safely and used to sew fine stitches.

The adult female population had very few luxuries but managed to make themselves glamorous by using all sorts of everyday things for make-up. Vinegar and, more rarely, eggs were used as a final rinse to make hair shine.

Mom started going grey when she was quite young; she was

probably only in her early thirties when her lovely dark brown hair started to fade. There was no hair dye as such available, but she did get hold of a packet of powder (probably clothes dye) that she dissolved with hot water in an old cracked basin.

Mom used to secretly daub her head with the mixture, using a well-worn toothbrush. Women didn't own up to dying their hair then, and she warned us not to mention it to anyone. The basin of dye was hidden in the pantry and kept on the go for many weeks.

There were no nylon stockings available at all, and women had to go bare-legged or wear socks when it was cold. Trousers had not come into fashion and were not worn at all by women, except for the Land Army girls. Some women, who were known as 'flighty', managed to get the occasional pair of stockings from American soldiers, but it was very much frowned upon, and rumour had it that the American servicemen expected favours in return. Most women coped by daubing their legs with gravy browning. They used to mix a spoonful of gravy powder in a bowl with some water and then very carefully paint it onto their legs. If they wanted seams in their stockings, as was the vogue in the 1940s, they would draw a line up the back of their legs with a brown or black eyebrow pencil. You needed a very steady hand for it – and definitely a good weather forecast! If it rained the gravy-powdered legs went very streaky.

After the end of the war, and whilst clothing rationing was still in place, women did begin to get the odd pair of nylon stockings, but they were very expensive. If they became laddered it was a major catastrophe. A clever entrepreneur set up a stocking mending business in Perry Barr. He had a very small shop, not much more than a kiosk, and acquired a machine with which he could repair nylons. It was rather like a small sewing machine with a little hooked needle. He would slide the damaged stocking under the hook and proceed to pick up the dropped stitch (or ladder) weaving nylon thread in and out until it was almost invisibly mended. For this he charged 6d.

Linda, Margaret and I were often sent down to Perry Barr with Mom or Aunty Doll's stockings to be repaired before they could go out. People throw tights and stockings away so casually now, but we spent many an hour sitting in that kiosk getting them mended – not once, not twice, but many times.

I do remember Mom having just one lipstick that she treasured. She only put a bit on her lips when she went out because it had to last such a long time. I remember that when it came to the end (there were no lip brushes then) she used to dip her little finger into the tube to get a bit more out and would lean close to the mirror and try to transfer the lipstick from her finger to her lips without smudging it. She called it making her Cupid's bow!

By the time I was eight or nine things were getting easier; clothes were no longer on ration and most foodstuffs were readily available again; we no longer had to queue for hours on end for bananas or our meat ration.

The legacy left to me by the war years is not the memory of bombs, injuries, War Office telegrams and deaths, but the fear of being confined in darkness, being suffocated, dreading being served certain kinds of food and an almost pathological concern about waste of any sort.

I am horrified when I see younger generations throwing away sauce bottles that are not completely empty. I still balance sauce bottles one on top of the other to get out those last few dregs. In the 1940s and early 1950s it was thought the greatest sin on earth to throw even the smallest piece of bread away – stale bread was used to make breadcrumbs for stuffing or treacle tart and mouldy bread went to feed the pigs.

If you should see me folding and storing used brown paper, the wrappings from bouquets, small pieces of string, the scrapings from margarine cartons and jam pots, cutting the mould from a piece of cheese, or gathering up small pieces of soap to reshape and reuse, I have not become mean or gone crazy; I am simply following the indisputable rules of my childhood: waste would help the Germans to win the war; waste was wicked; waste would not be tolerated; waste would be punished.

The In-laws and the Outlaws

I belonged to a typically large and close-knit family of the 1940s. There were numerous aunts, uncles and cousins, and we spent many happy hours in each other's houses. That doesn't seem to happen today with families; perhaps television, cars and holidays abroad are the reason for this change. People are able to look outside their immediate family circle for entertainment, support, friendship and amusement.

Mom had four sisters – Lily, Jessie, Violet and Dorothy (Doll) – and a brother, Percy. Dad had two sisters – Kathleen and Muriel.

Aunt Doll and her husband, Frank, had three children – Margaret, Roger and Susan. We spent our earliest years with this branch of the family in a house that we all shared. Aunt Doll and Uncle Frank were great characters, full of fun and very happily married. It wasn't revealed until they reached their golden wedding that theirs had been a shotgun wedding. Their actual wedding date was three months later than had always been believed. Aunt Doll, in her matter-of-fact way, thought it was silly to continue with a fifty-year-old secret in today's easier moral climate and took the opportunity to set the record straight with her children. I wonder if Grandad knew or if Grandma – bless her – kept the secret from him and covered Margaret's early arrival as that of a premature baby!

Uncle Frank was a great hypochondriac, but funny with it. He read the medical encyclopaedia regularly, searching for symptoms. I remember he did have a troublesome hernia and often had indigestion. Aunt Doll would dash about the house shouting, 'Has anybody got a mint imp?' (Mint Imperial.) I believe that Uncle Frank suffered from quite serious depression now and again, but this was not dwelt upon and only talked about quietly from time to time amongst the grown-ups. Uncle Frank died quite recently as the result of a stroke when he was well into his eighties.

Frank had his own removal business and stored his big furniture van across the road at his brother's. As well as private removals, he did a lot of contract work for the famous furniture store, Restalls. He often bought home quite nice bits of furniture that people no longer wanted. I think this may have been the origin of many of the mismatched chairs which graced Aunt Doll's back kitchen.

The removal van was used for other purposes, too. We all belonged to the Brownies, and every year Uncle Frank's furniture wagon was commandeered to take the Brownies and their equipment to camp. Some thirty to forty Brownies sat in the back of the wagon on blankets on the floor, surrounded by tents and boxes of food – seat belts were a thing of the future. Aunt Doll has some wonderful old cine film of us setting off. All you can see over the tailboard of the wagon are our tiny smiling faces topped by Brownie berets.

Aunt Doll appeared to have a stronger personality than Uncle Frank. She had then, and still has now, a very determined character. There is nothing wishy-washy about Aunt Doll – she always seemed to know what she wanted and how to get it.

I don't remember her going out to work, but she had to look after the removal business from home as far as bookings and accounts were concerned. She also worked hard at supplementing the family income with different moneymaking schemes. She was an extremely good dressmaker and spent many hours on an old treadle sewing machine making everything from dance frocks to curtains.

Aunt Doll was a great one for keeping up with the fashions, and each spring she had a brand new outfit – everything – coat, hat, handbag, gloves, shoes, dress, and often jewellery too. Mom used to get a bit envious; I don't think she really begrudged her sister but would have liked the odd new dress herself.

I think Aunt Doll was the glamour puss of all my aunts. She was always trying different diets in order to stay slim and experimenting with anything new in the hairdressing line. She did everybody's hair in the back kitchen, using whatever latest hairdressing gadgets she had acquired. I well remember ringlets, when long strips of rag were wrapped round and round my waist-length hair to make it curl, and horrible metal crimpers with sharp teeth which were snapped on my head to make Marcel waves. Vinegar and occasionally eggs were used as a rinse after thoroughly washing the hair with hard green soap.

Margaret lives in Canada with her husband, John. They have no children, but own an idyllic holiday resort, part of the Thousand Islands, on the St Lawrence River. They are busy with guests during the summer, but when the Canadian winter arrives they return to their warmer home in Florida.

Roger lives in the Midlands with his wife, Anita. They have one daughter, Tracey. Sadly, Tracey has cystic fibrosis but she is a little fighter and leads as normal a life as possible, with great courage.

Susan, too, lives in the Midlands with her partner. They have a daughter, Hayley. Interestingly, Susan works at Aston Villa Football Club – the very club with which our grandfather had been involved for so many years in the first half of the century.

Once things settled down after the war, and Dad was at home for longer periods of time, we started spending holidays with Mom's only brother, Percy, his wife, Lil, and their adopted daughter, Pamela.

Uncle Percy was quite a character and a very hard-working chap. He followed in his father's footsteps as far as gardening was concerned and had the most wonderful vegetable garden – a huge plot that provided for all his family's needs from year end to year end.

He came regularly to our house at Aldridge Road to help with the vegetable plot. Dad was often away, and Mom couldn't cope with the garden as well as four small children. The vegetable plot couldn't be left to grass because there was a desperate need to supplement food supplies at this early stage after the war.

Uncle Percy had two jobs. He used to get up at four o'clock in the morning to call at several farms around Lichfield collecting the milk in big silver churns which he lifted into the back of his huge milk wagon. He travelled with the milk from Lichfield to Birmingham, dropping the churns off at Handsworth Dairies. Following this he travelled to his day job at Wolf's, where work began at 7 a.m. Wolf's were famous in Birmingham for making drills long before anybody had heard of Black & Decker. Many in the family are still using drills which came from Wolf's more than fifty years ago. At the end of the day, Uncle Percy would return to Handsworth Dairies, pick up the sterilised churns and deliver them back to the farms around Lichfield. He must have been a strong and energetic man, but never appeared so to me; I don't ever remember him rushing or getting agitated about anything.

Dad and Uncle Percy were real mates and always helped each other with any jobs that were too big to tackle alone. They developed a wonderful signalling system if they needed to speak to each other urgently. There were very few houses with telephones at that time and the only way of getting in touch was by letter. Uncle Percy had to pass our house in Aldridge Road each day on his way to Birmingham. If Dad wanted to speak to him he would lean our big blackboard against a tree stump at the side of the road bordering our house. When the blackboard was in place Dad would chalk messages on it in foot-high letters such as 'Percy – call in' or 'Percy – bring the big drill over' or 'Percy – could you put the potatoes in next week?'

A strange thing about Uncle Percy was that whenever we went out for the day or on holiday he always got wet. It was a family joke that we could never get Uncle Percy home dry. He would fall in a stream, or spill water from the kettle when making tea, or get splashed with boiling water from the radiator, or spill a bottle of milk down his front; the list of ways for him to get wet was endless. Maybe it stemmed from the famous story of when he was a small boy. Percy climbed onto the wash boiler when it was full of steaming hot water and fell in head first, almost drowning in the sudsy water. He had to be fished out and virtually hung up to dry!

Dad found one or two of Uncle Percy's traits really aggravating. When we went for a day out Dad would lead the way in our car, with Uncle Percy following behind. He was a bit of a miser so when we came to even the smallest downward hill, Uncle Percy would switch off his engine, put the car into neutral and coast down the hill to save petrol. Of course, this meant he kept falling behind and we had to wait for him to catch up. Additionally, he would not put his car lights on until it was really dark – it was almost as though he thought he was saving money on his household electricity bill by this behaviour.

However, this miserliness stood our family in very good stead because Uncle Percy was always willing to lend the money he had accumulated when major purchases were planned. He was our banker for many years when items such as replacement cars, washing machines or college support were needed. I think he really missed Dad when he died and kept a watchful eye on us girls for many years afterwards, always being there with ready cash if we needed it.

Aunt Lil was a great character too, in her own way. A sorrow in her life was that she could not have children of her own. However, she did eventually adopt a little girl of just a few weeks old whom she called Pamela. Pamela was a much-loved only child, although brought up very strictly by Aunt Lil, and without the rough and tumble of family life, which we enjoyed. Happily, Pamela spent most weekends and holidays with us, so she did have the benefit of siblings of a sort.

Aunt Lil was a fantastic housekeeper and had received her training firstly as a downstairs maid, and then as a parlourmaid at a big house in Handsworth. She often told us stories about her life as a maid, of how she had to get up at dawn to scrub the steps, to clear the ashes and blacklead the grates before anyone in the household was awake. She also learned how to do the most beautiful laundry. No one I have ever known could peg out a line of washing as beautiful as Aunt Lil's. The whiteness was startling, and the quality of her starching and ironing had to be seen to be believed.

Her house was spotless and done through every day of the week to a strict routine. She used a long thin knitting needle to poke bits of fluff out from under the skirting board, and balls of scrunched up newspaper to polish her windows. The kitchen floor was polished with red Cardinal wax until you could see your face in it. All the saucepans were cleaned and scoured to within an inch of their lives and hung up in neat rows in the pantry.

Aunt Lil's teas were legendary. Aunt Lil and Mom took it in turns to do Sunday tea. Mom always put on a good spread and was used to catering for a big family, but Aunt Lil had been taught, whilst in service, about the rights and wrongs of

Sunday tea, and this made the difference.

The table would be set with a damask cloth with a felt mat underneath to protect the polish. The best china would be used; this was brightly coloured, decorated with a mixture of red, blue and gold. Cutlery from the canteen was used rather than that from the kitchen drawer.

We would each be served with slices of home-cooked breaded ham and tongue on a large china plate. To add to this would be salad from the garden – lettuce, radish, cucumber, tomatoes and thinly sliced Spanish onion soaked in vinegar. Little side dishes contained beetroot, red cabbage, pickled gherkins, brown-skinned onions, piccalilli and sticky brown chutney. There would be a huge plate of the thinnest bread and butter imaginable. Plates of home-made pork pie, hard-boiled or Scotch eggs and a variety of cheeses, such as English Cheddar, Wensleydale, Caerphilly, Red Leicester, Gorgonzola, Edam and Danish blue would complete the first course.

When all had been devoured and the plates cleared away, the excitement would mount because we knew the *pièce de résistance* would arrive in a moment. Aunt Lil made the most superb trifles in the world; huge things presented in the most gorgeous glass bowls, decorated magnificently with cream and chocolate shavings and beautiful black cherries oozing with juice. I am supposed to be pretty good at making trifles, too, but they cannot compare with those remembered from Aunt Lil's teas.

After the trifle came the cakes! Coconut pyramids with a cherry on the top, rock buns packed with fruit, almond slices that melted in your mouth, big fruit cakes decorated with toasted nuts, macaroons with rice paper on the bottom, Swiss roll filled with home-made raspberry jam and sprinkled with sugar, lemon curd tartlets, butterfly cakes packed with cream, and sweet, sticky treacle tart. How Aunt Lil achieved what she did with limited food supplies I just don't know, but her teas were the highlight of our young lives, and are still remembered and talked about to this day. When Linda was devastated by unhappy events in her life she always asked Mom to arrange for Aunt Lil to do her a tea; she always did and it always lifted Linda's spirits. Maybe it was comfort eating, but it worked.

Whenever we went on a holiday, Aunt Lil would have Pamela's clothes washed, pressed, starched and packed so neatly – she was always immaculate. Mom normally had our clothes clean, but they were carelessly jumbled together in the big aluminium suitcase. Aunt Lil took their picnic with individual packets of sandwiches nicely wrapped in greaseproof paper, with plates and forks and cups to use. Our sandwiches were stuffed into an old cornflake packet, not too well shaken out, and rather squashed by the time we got to eat them. Aunt Lil was generous and always took a few extra bits for her ever-hungry nieces.

I think Uncle Percy and Aunt Lil were a little disappointed at Pamela's choice of marriage partner, and, as it turned out, Pamela and her husband parted, leaving Pam with four young children to bring up alone.

Pamela had not been allowed to learn any housewifery skills from her mother. Absolutely nobody could match Aunt Lil's accomplishments, and Pamela didn't even try. Consequently she has always lived in the most glorious mess with the most gloriously happy children.

After her adoptive parents' death, Pamela traced her birth mother and learned about why she was given up for adoption. She discovered that she has many half-brothers and sisters, and one full brother, and is now in contact with them all. She was lucky enough to discover that her birth mother was still alive, although very old and ailing. Sadly, her birth mother has since died, but Pamela had a couple of happy years with her, catching up on their fifty years of separation and their feelings for each other.

Mom's oldest sister, Jess, left home when she married Jack, and they set up home in Great Barr. Jack was a master butcher and had his own shop in Thornbridge Avenue. It was marvellous to stay with Aunt Jess because you always got meat for your dinner! Even their cat, Fluff, had stewing steak every day in his dish. I can remember staying with Aunt Jess once when she put a great big steaming dish of tripe and onions in front of me – I think I was about five. I just stared at this unbelievable mass of white, jelly-like substance and was immediately sick straight into the bowl! Aunt Jess was really cross, but I didn't care – it looked like a jellyfish to me, and I couldn't imagine eating it.

Another very vivid memory of staying with Aunt Jess was when she gave me a lollipop, which was triangular in shape and made of boiled sweet substance. I pushed it into my mouth and then couldn't pull it out again; because of the design, it got stuck behind my teeth. I started to panic and then choke but neither Aunt Jess nor I could get it out of my mouth. Aunt Jess started to panic, too, and rushed out to the tool shed for a hammer. I well remember the pain of her hitting my cheeks to break the lollipop up whilst it was still in my mouth. It didn't break, but just caused my cheeks to bleed inside and add to my discomfort. Of course, the lollipop began very slowly to dissolve and we managed to get it out.

Aunt Jess and Uncle Jack had two children, John and Loretta. They were much older than all the other children in the family and we admired and looked up to them. John was an apprentice and was learning to be a cabinetmaker, but in his spare time his hobby was collecting birds' eggs. I don't think it was illegal at that particular time, and John had a large collection of eggs displayed attractively in glass cases. I was threatened with all sorts of torture if I touched them.

Whenever I went to stay, if John was at home he used to take me over the fence at the end of their garden onto the tip. Every kind of rubbish was dumped on the tip and we were not supposed to climb on there, but I loved it.

All sorts of things could be found that were really attractive to a small child – little bits of coloured glass, buttons, doll's heads, clay pipes, fish paste jars and pots, and, occasionally, bits of jewellery. There was also a lot of ash from household fires tipped there and we used to come in after one of these adventures as black as the grate. Aunt Jess didn't have a bathroom, so it was into the kitchen sink for a strip wash and a good telling off.

I loved Loretta; she was so beautiful. She had the most wonderful golden hair and smiling face. I watched entranced when she got dressed up to go out in the latest fashion of the early fifties; she wore make-up and high heels and her petticoats stuck out for miles underneath her dance frocks. My dream came true when she asked me to be the one and only bridesmaid at her wedding. She was the most beautiful fairy-tale bride, and I was part of it in a pink satin frock with a scalloped hemline and crinoline skirt.

Real tragedy struck this branch of the family, and it causes me anguish when I think of it. Aunt Jess and Uncle Jack both died as a result of a car crash on their way home from a day out; they were in their early sixties.

Very soon afterwards Loretta was diagnosed as having leukaemia and died extremely quickly, leaving two young sons. She struggled bravely until the day she died to care for her children, manoeuvring herself around the house as best she could to look after her boys during her very weakest final days.

I think I shall remember for ever a lovely sunny summer's day when Loretta and I were skipping along Thornbridge Avenue holding hands and singing, as loudly as we could, 'Oh, what a beautiful morning!' We were really happy that day.

I see Loretta's sons occasionally. They have both grown up into the most attractive and good-natured young men, of whom she would be immensely proud.

Another of Mom's sisters, Aunt Lil, was much more remote. She married a talented cabinetmaker (Harry), and moved away from the rest of the family to Quinton. I don't know whether it was the geographical distance, or Uncle Harry's nervousness of social occasions, that caused this remoteness. Of course, we did see each other from time to time, but visits were planned rather than spontaneous. Whenever Uncle Harry visited us, he would never take his coat off and sat on the very edge of his chair in a most uncomfortable manner. I think he must have been dreadfully shy.

Aunt Lil had the sadness of losing her first baby only hours after he was born and this caused her to overprotect her next child, Henry. From an early age he showed he was going to be an unusual and solitary child.

He didn't take up any of the normal boy's hobbies such as football or cricket, or collecting birds' eggs, or making trolleys, or marbles, or just roaming around the streets playing tag or jacks or fivestones. No, Henry learned to play the accordion, collected bus tickets to stick in albums, and mostly stayed indoors reading his comics and following solitary pursuits.

I, of all his cousins, went to stay with him for the odd weekend. I cannot to this day remember how we occupied ourselves or what games we played. Aunt Lil and Uncle Harry seemed really old (and old-fashioned) parents to me.

On one famous occasion when I was staying at Number 91, Henry and I were playing upstairs. I decided to go downstairs and missed my footing, falling from the top of the stairs to the very bottom, landing with a thud against a cupboard. Aunt Lil came rushing from the kitchen in a dreadful state. She saw me lying in a bloody heap at the bottom of the stairs, and without a moment's hesitation said, 'Oh, my God – I thought it was Henry!' I had no lasting ill effects from the fall, but the family has lived on the story for years; it causes great merriment.

For whatever reason, this branch of the family didn't figure large in our lives, but there are several enduring memories, especially of Aunt Lil. She never forgot our birthdays, and all her nieces and nephews got a card with a half-crown in it every year until they were fifteen – a fabulous sum to us in those days, when the average weekly pocket money was about threepence (less than two new pence).

Aunt Lil was also renowned for making both simnel cake and caraway seed cake. The first I loved, the second I couldn't bear as a child, and I don't care much for it now.

And a third memory: Aunt Lil was adamant that the whole room would look tidy if the ashes were cleared and the grate polished as soon as you got up in the morning. She always did this in her own home and in anyone else's home that she happened to be visiting – whether invited to or not!

Henry is still a very different sort of person. He lives in Hong Kong and, in his forties, married a Taiwanese bride. I met her once and found her charming. At first, I thought her subservience to Henry a little disturbing, but quickly came to understand that this was a cultural difference – not slavery!

Aunty Vi was the lively one of the family, and was 'tutted' upon occasionally by Mom and my other aunts. She married a really lovely man, Fred, whose family came from Aston in Birmingham. Fred was a kind and cheerful character who loved his family and worked hard. He and Vi were the life and soul of family parties. All the children of the family loved Uncle Fred and Aunt Vi to be present at the celebrations, but the grown-ups sometimes tried to quieten them down a bit.

For instance, at one of our Christmas parties Aunty Vi had a few sherries too many and started disrobing. Mom was scandalised and tried to get Uncle Fred and Dad to stop her, but she wouldn't stop until she got down to her all-in-one corselets, upon which she was removed unceremoniously from the room. We children loved it – we had never seen anyone undressed before. I have to say that girls now go to the clubs in town with a lot less covering them than Aunt Vi's voluminous salmon-pink undergarments.

Aunt Vi and Uncle Fred enlivened many a Christmas and birthday party with their rendition of 'Knees Up, Mother Brown', complete with actions. They also impersonated Fred Astaire and Ginger Rogers doing the Charleston – Uncle Fred was a brilliant tap-dancer and had a similar physique to Fred Astaire.

Uncle Fred's magical musical performance when playing the spoons caused much hilarity, too. He would take two dessert spoons from the kitchen drawer and then, by holding them back-to-back in a certain manner, would deliver a very good tune, rather in the way that castanets are played. He would tap the spoons all over his body, from the top of his head to the soles of his feet, accompanied by lively jigging and clapping from the rest of the party.

Uncle Fred remained cheerful throughout his long marriage to Aunt Vi, despite some difficult years. Aunt Vi suffered with an illness that would probably now be recognised as severe post-natal depression, causing her to spend frequent spells in hospital.

Uncle Fred dealt with it all with great good humour – sometimes at Aunt Vi's expense. But we all knew how much he really cared for her, and that he was using a kind of defensive and typical 'Brummie' humour to get him through the rough patches.

Uncle Fred and Aunt Vi had two daughters, Anne and Christine. Anne had two children and two grandchildren. She has borne, bravely, the early loss of her young son, Michael, as well as witnessing the struggles of her beautiful granddaughter with autism. Christine and her husband run a busy corner shop in Ward End.

Uncle Fred was a painter and decorator, and a very good one too. He did all the decorating in the family and I can see him now in his white overalls mixing up big buckets of foul-smelling fish glue and doing a tightrope walk across a long plank stretched between two sets of steps to paper a ceiling. I can see him, too, with a huge pair of scissors, trimming along the edge of rolls of wallpaper. Wallpaper didn't come ready trimmed, so if you didn't have a very steady hand when doing the cutting, there would be gaps between the strips when they were stuck on the wall.

Uncle Fred died some years ago, but when I think of him I have two particular memories. Firstly, he always grew the most beautiful cornflowers in his garden: rows and rows of really bright blues and pinks, and I loved them. Aunt Vi is still living in the same house, and those cornflowers are still coming up fifty years on.

Secondly, Uncle Fred loved playing with his little nieces and nephews, but was sometimes a bit rough and dangerous. His favourite game was to pick us up and throw us up to the ceiling to make us squeal. Of course, more than once we received a good crack from the ceiling and would end up in tears. But, childlike, after a few minutes we would want to have another turn. Cries of 'Stop it, Fred, put her down! You'll damage her brain!' came from our worried moms. I don't think the bumps and bangs did us any lasting harm!

Aunt Vi seems to go from strength to strength. In later life all her health problems have disappeared and she is an amusing and interesting lady of almost ninety-two. She is as sharp as a razor and knows exactly what is going on. She loves to watch television and I think this keeps her up to date. She still has a wicked sense of humour.

Aunt Vi and her family are hard-working, down-to-earth 'Brummies'. Academic subjects have not appealed to them, but they have common sense in bucketloads and are more straightforwardly honest than a lot of people who consider themselves 'professional middle class'. I learned valuable lessons from sharing my childhood years with such a diverse family. I know for certain that we all experience the same joys and sorrows and value family life highly.

I never knew Dad's sister, Muriel, for whom I was named. She died when she was barely eighteen years old. We had always been told that she had died due to blood poisoning caused by an abscess on a tooth. It wasn't until I found her death certificate quite recently that I discovered that the cause of her death was leukaemia.

Dad rarely spoke of her; I didn't realise until adulthood that his seeming indifference covered a deep and overwhelming grief for the loss of his sister. He was barely sixteen when she died. I imagine that he was told, 'Boys don't cry,' and so had to hide his grief and unhappiness inside himself.

I know this experience had a profound effect on Dad because I rarely remember him showing either emotion or open affection. I was devastated by being told, at about the age of six, that I was too old to be kissed goodnight anymore. I can still feel the pain and bewilderment of being gently, but firmly, pushed away by him with the flat of his hand.

Dad's other sister, Kath, has always been a mystery. I gather from looking through old photo albums that she was a popular and talented child. There are many pictures of her taking part in amateur theatre productions of Shakespeare plays, as well as evidence of her musical and literary talents. And then, suddenly, it all stops. From about the age of twenty, there are no more pictures or mention of Aunt Kath anywhere.[1]

From a very early age I knew that Aunt Kath was *persona non grata*. Even Dad could barely speak her name. I do know that she joined the Red Cross during the war and later emigrated to America, living there until she died in her seventies.

We did begin to receive the occasional typed, rather formal, airmail letter from her after the war, to which I assume Dad replied. Sadly she died alone in America with not a single relative from her homeland in England present at her funeral. She found kindness in her final years from a chapter of Hell's Angels who lived next door to her in San Francisco, and devoted companionship from her beloved dog, Charles.

How sad that Dad lost one sister to leukaemia and another due to banishment from the family for an unknown 'sin'. There may be a postscript to this chapter if I can persuade one of my two remaining elderly aunts to unravel this lifelong mystery before they die. I have asked Mom to explain it many times but she remains tight-lipped. [2]

These then were my aunts and uncles. They were all so very different from one another, but they were always there in the midst of my growing-up years; I expect I took our close-knit family circle for granted, not valuing it as I should. It is only now in the 1990s when I work with so many disjointed, dysfunctional and isolated young people that I realise how extremely lucky I have been. Yes, every branch of the family experienced real tragedy, but there was always someone there to wipe away your tears, to help pick up the pieces and to support and love you until your pain was eased.

---

[1] In 2003, Mom finally told me that Aunt Kath had become involved with a boy much younger than herself. She used to be seen kissing and canoodling on a bench and the neighbourhood was scandalised. It was rumoured that she became pregnant – an unimaginable event at the time (1928) for a single girl. The boy's parents were furious – they accused her of ruining his chances in life and leading him astray, and were adamant that they would not allow their association to continue. Mom was unsure or unwilling to say whether the pregnancy was terminated or whether the baby was adopted. I have tried to confirm this story with Aunt Doll, but she says she has never heard it before. So is it true or has Mom's dementia and Aunt Doll's old age muddied the waters? I don't see how we can ever know.

[2] Since completing this chapter, several of the in-laws and the outlaws, including my mother, have left us. Aunt Doll, at ninety-three, is the sole reminder of her generation – and is treasured by us all.

Sadly, we have also said goodbye to John (Margaret's husband), and to Tracey (Roger and Anita's daughter).

Grandad Ross, Grandmother Fanny Ross and family, 1914. Middle row (left to right): Auntie Vi and Uncle Percy. Front row (left to right): Auntie Jess, Auntie Lil and Ivy (The author's mother). Fanny was expecting Auntie Doll.

The Bridgewater children, 1916.
Left to right: Auntie Kath, Auntie Muriel and Kenneth (The author's father).

Saturday shopping in Perry Barr.
Little had changed since this much earlier photograph from 1912.

Linda and Muriel in 1943,
after their evacuation to Lampwit Major, South Wales.

The author, Muriel, in 1945 (aged 3).
A happy smile – war is over, peace is declared.

Grandma and Grandad Ross in their garden
at Ivy Cottage, 176 Birmingham Road, Lichfield.

The war is over – together again in Blackpool, 1946.
Back row (left to right): Uncle Percy, Auntie Lil, Mom and Dad.
Front row (left to right): Cousin Pam, Linda, Muriel and Lorna.

The bench in the garden of 172 Aldridge Road.
Left to right: Jennifer, Lorna, Muriel, Linda, Mom and Dad.

The Bench near the end of its days.

The mangle – otherwise known as 'The Wringer'.

36 Livingstone Road, Handsworth, Birmingham,
photographed in 2002.

Uncle Albert Sweetman's house (opposite number 36).
The road between the houses was the children's playground.

Westminster Road Infant School,
photograph taken in 2002.

A trip in the Austin 7 – taking a tea break, 1946.
Left to right: Muriel, Lorna and Linda.

Climbing Dinas Mawddwy in the Austin 7.

On the seafront in Wales with the cowhide bag.
Left to right: Linda (with bag), Lorna, Dad and Muriel.

Linda and Muriel in their 'best' knickers.

A happy photograph taken at Burnham-on-Sea in 1951, prior to the trauma of our near drowning. Left to right: Lorna, Linda, Muriel, Mom and Jennifer.

Outside Buckingham Palace in London to see the decorations for the coronation after watching the ceremony on Auntie Doll's nine-inch, black-and-white TV. Left to right: Muriel, Linda, Jennifer, Mom and Lorna.

Happy Holidays in 1953.
Left to right: Linda, Mom, Dad, Jennifer and Muriel, with Lorna (front).

Off to Guide camp in Uncle Frank's removal van.
Westminster Road Congregational Church is in the background.

172 Aldridge Road.
The wall, built by Muriel's father, was much admired. The shed roof is just visible
over the gate, and the parked VW Beetle was used on an early European tour.

Mom in the side entry with Tibby on her shoulder.
In the background, the shed roof – our launch pad.

Linda, Muriel, Lorna and Jennifer on the swing in the garden at 172 Aldridge Road.
Mrs Harvey's hen house is in the background.

Another view of the shed, during the winter of 1953.
Note the coke bunker at the end of the shed, and the bench.

The cross channel ferry (Dover to Calais) – our first trip abroad, 1955.
Left to right: Dad, Pam, Auntie Lil, Lorna, Linda, Mom, Muriel, Jen and Uncle Percy.

The Simplon pass over the Alps, 1953. Left to right: Auntie Lil, Pam, Linda,
Lorna, Mom and Muriel, with Jennifer and Uncle Percy in front.

Church Anniversary dresses made by Linda.
Left to right: Muriel, Jennifer, Lorna and Linda.

Nits, Ringworm and Hands on Heads

I cannot remember my first day at school. I do remember being very small, very tired and very lonely for a long time. Memories of my first classroom are extremely vague; I remember that the windows were very high up and I was unable to see out of them. Precious things, such as coloured chalks, were kept on the windowsills out of the way of little fingers. The first school that I attended was Westminster Road in Handsworth, which was just a short walk away from where we lived in Livingstone Road.

Good memories of my first year at school are very few. I loved getting our little bottle of milk with a drinking straw. It is hard to believe now that a straw was such a novelty, and to have the whole third of a pint of milk each was an amazing luxury after the deprivation and shortages of the war years. On really cold winter days the crate containing our milk was dragged across the floor to stand in the hearth by the fire. Yes, we did have a real coal fire in the corner of our classroom, surrounded by a huge black fireguard. There was a bucket of coal nearby to make up the fire as and when necessary. Some teachers were motherly and kind and let us put our hats and gloves to warm when it was bitterly cold.

In the afternoons we were allowed to put our heads on our desks to have a little sleep – and all slept very soundly. I have very fleeting memories of the playground, and this is where I experienced great loneliness – a 'left out' feeling. I didn't understand the games, the rules or the cliques, and I was always cold.

As far as learning was concerned, I could read before I went to school and do not remember struggling with this subject at all. Grandma Rose was very good at reading with us. She came every week to visit and would take us onto her lap, give us a dolly mixture out of an old Gold Leaf tobacco tin, let us look at her lovely marcasite brooches, try on her ruby and diamond rings and then read to us. How cleverly she instilled in us the association between pleasure and reading.

I think I could write my name, too, and always enjoyed having a piece of chalk and a little slate on which to practise my letters. We each had a disgusting piece of cloth which we used to wipe our slates. I didn't often have a hanky to take to school – no tissues in those days – so I used my chalk rag as an alternative to my sleeve when I had a runny nose! When we were not using our slates we had pieces of charcoal and a small scrap of paper to either draw or write upon. The charcoal was very brittle, made from wood that had been slowly burned. It made a rather horrid scratchy noise on the paper and your fingers became exceedingly dirty; still, that good old chalk rag-cum-nose-wiper served yet another useful purpose.

Plasticine was another delight. We had little wooden boards to roll it out on, and if we were really lucky got recognisable coloured balls of it to play with. This only happened at the beginning of term when new stocks were issued. We had white, yellow, green, pink, blue and orange to choose from. After a very short time we had to be satisfied with a dull brownish grey mixture because we couldn't keep the colours separated for long. I always thought the plasticine smelled lovely, whatever its colour, and I still like the smell now.

In reception class I can remember making a windmill and a clock. The windmill was simply a square of paper with the corners folded in to the middle, pinned securely in the centre and attached to a stick. The clock was a circle of card with a hole punched in the middle, through which the fingers were secured with a butterfly clip. We had numbers cut out of sticky coloured paper to glue in the correct places. This craftwork must have impressed me, for I think about the clock and the windmill often. I also remember absolutely gorgeous coloured sticky paper that we were allowed to cut into shapes to make people, flowers, cars, birds and suchlike. We had strict instructions not to waste the tiniest bit of it. The glue tasted lovely.

We were punished for the slightest misdemeanour. Really serious offences meant you had to go to the front, hold out your hand and get a good hard tap with the ruler. This terrified me and I never committed so grave an offence that I received this punishment. Lesser sins were punished by either having to stand in the corner or outside the classroom door for what seemed a very long time. A general punishment, used when the teacher could not decide who was talking or fidgeting, was for the whole class to sit bolt upright with hands on heads. I expect this lasted for barely five minutes, but seemed much longer and it certainly made our arms ache dreadfully.

After only a very short time at Westminster Road, we moved house and Linda and I had to transfer to another infant school called Birchfield Road Primary School. My memories of this school are much clearer and I can look back with more affection.

Birchfield Road was a small village school in Perry Barr on the site where the University of Central England now stands. It is hard to believe that the huge buildings that now house hundreds of university students occupy the same site that was our playground and our school. The school was divided into three sections: infant boys and girls combined, junior boys and junior girls. As infants, when we went outside to play, we could hear the big boys and girls playing on the other side of high dividing walls – the boys to the right and the girls to the left of our playground. We longed to join them.

We had no indoor toilets and had to remember to use the toilets in the playground at playtime, because it caused so much trouble if you needed to go during lesson time. Many children would wet their pants rather than ask to be taken outside during the lesson because of derisory jeers from other children.

Linda and I had been well warned before we started at Birchfield Road that we had to be well-behaved, clever and willing pupils. One of the teachers in the infants' section of the school was a lifelong friend of our paternal grandmother, and her reputation had gone before her. Although Grandma Rose was now dead we still thought a bad report from this particular teacher would get through to her and we would be in serious trouble. When Grandma was alive we were in awe of her and we weren't exactly sure what 'dead' meant. Did she still have the necessary powers to punish us? I managed nearly always to be good, but Linda had quite a few close shaves with the ruler.

I did do one very wrong thing when I first attended Birchfield Road, together with my friend Janet. We were asked by our teacher to go into a little washroom at the side of the hall to 'fetch a jar of paste'. We thought our teacher said, 'Go and wash out the jar of paste.' Janet and I couldn't understand this because the jar of paste was brand new and waste of any kind in our childhood was a really serious crime for which you could expect to be punished severely. The paste was extremely difficult to get out of the jar, which was pyramid shaped with a brush stuck tightly through a hole in the lid. Janet and I took it in turns to try to wash the paste from the jar and I can remember us crying with frustration at how difficult it was; we dared not go back to the classroom until it was done.

Horror of horrors – when we took the gleaming jar back to the classroom our teacher said, 'What have you done with that paste – it was a new jar!' I was nearly sick with fright, hung my head and muttered that the jar was empty when we found it. Janet agreed. The teacher marched us to the washroom and examined the sink and the little bits of paper from the label in the plughole. She gave us a very steely look but couldn't prove conclusively what we had done. I am sure she knew, though, and probably got into trouble herself for wasting supplies.

I wasn't so lonely at this school because I made several good friends – Bronwyn, Janet, Clemency, Duree, Patricia and Brenda. Bronwyn was my very first close friend when I was about six. We spent all our time together when I started at this school and went for tea at each other's houses. I can still feel my hurt and bewilderment when her family decided they were emigrating to Australia. Bronwyn and I both cried and cried and talked constantly about the big ship she would be going on and how long it would take and whether it would sink. There was a big publicity drive in the early 1950s for people to go to Australia, where all sorts of professions were desperately needed. There was a scheme whereby you could emigrate for just £10.

I am sure they have had a good life in Australia but even now when I hear children playing and singing 'The big ship sails on the alley-alley-o' I get a lump in my throat. After Bronwyn, I took up with a group of friends; my childish logic must have sensed this would be safer than having one special friend.

Janet was a sad little thing because she had been born with a very deformed leg and had to wear an iron frame with a big boot to strengthen and lengthen her leg. She was clever, though, and very plucky, and our little gang always looked out for her. We felt sorry that there were so many things she couldn't take part in such as games, playtime, dancing and even sitting on the floor in assembly. I don't know what became of her when we left junior school, but she did pass for grammar school, as did the rest of our gang.

Brenda was Scottish and used to lend me the most fabulous comics called *Oor Wullie* with many stories in them about 'The Broons'. We sometimes managed to get a copy of the *Dandy*, the *Beano* or the *Buster* if we were lucky. Mom and Dad didn't approve of comics, and we could only read them occasionally when they came our way second-hand from cousin Henry. Together with Patricia, Brenda and I spent lots of after-school time and weekends playing together. I don't know how old we would have been at this time, but I do know a lot of our games were played in Patricia's garden shed and involved doctors and nurses! Some things never change!

Clemency was a lovely friend, both in spirit and in looks. She was fragile and blond and gentle – she looked like I imagined fairies would look. I was her special friend and she clung to me all through our early years at school. I was shy and quiet too, and she must have felt safe with me.

When we were small there was no vaccine for polio, and we were forbidden to swim in dirty water because there was a very real chance of contracting the waterborne polio virus. Clemency became very ill one day and it was quickly realised that she had polio. To avoid death she had to be placed in an iron lung, which breathed for her. The machine was hideous – a great iron casement into which they put her slim little body with only her head visible. She lay on her back in this contraption for months and months. All her lovely golden hair was worn away on the back of her head; she couldn't move, eat or speak, and had no way of easing the hours, weeks and months of terror. Mom used to take me on the long journey to visit her as often as she could, and I would sit at the side of the iron lung on a chair whilst Clemency looked straight above her and through a series of cleverly placed mirrors so that she could see me without turning her head.

Eventually she did come home to be nursed and to convalesce. Her mother was a fantastically strong and supportive person and was determined that Clemency would recover as fully as possible. She massaged and exercised her daughter's wasted limbs for hours on end.

Clemency overcame this awful illness with extreme courage, but growth was restricted on one side of her body, causing her a lifelong limp. Her beautiful hair grew again and she peacefully accepted her lot. I remained fast friends with her and never minded that we could no longer play outdoors or run and skip. Sadly, when we moved away from Birmingham I lost touch with her, but I did hear a rumour that she had met and married a lovely man; I do hope the rumour was true.

Duree was my most outrageous friend. She had really exotic looks – very dark, thick curly hair and flashing, almost black, eyes. And she was rich! Unusually for those days, both her parents worked. Her father was a director of a company and her mother was a nursing sister. They lived in a really nice house with fitted wardrobes! The significance of this may be lost on the present generation, but almost everyone you knew had dark brown, cumbersome, utility furniture. And, even more amazing, Duree's mother had more than one pair of shoes! In fact, she had a whole row, and we were allowed to try them on – absolute bliss!

Duree was the only friend I ever went to stay the night with, and I could never get over the fact that she didn't have to share a bedroom with anyone, was allowed snacks in her room, could jump on the bed, use the telephone, had her own radio, had her own box of coloured pencils, could answer back... and found it normal that her mother smoked cigarettes. We remained close friends until we went our separate ways to grammar school.

Duree died in an accident whilst very young. She was a passenger in a car travelling along Chester Road North in Sutton when a vehicle suddenly pulled out from a hotel car park and hit them. Although Duree had no mark on her, she was found to be dead in the car; it was discovered that she had broken her neck. She was twenty years old.

Of course, when this little gang was at school we were happy and cheerful and it is a blessing you cannot see what lies ahead. We had many happy years playing and working together. Each playtime we decided what we would do. Sometimes we played simple games such as ring-a-ring-o'-roses or Lucy Lockett's lost her pocket. Other games were a bit more complicated because you had to decide who was 'on', for example, in blind man's buff. We also played skipping and ball games, hoops, hopscotch, whip and top and, in the appropriate season, conkers, 'marlies' and jacks or fivestones.

I remember being bullied to the point of tears by one horrid girl when I was about eight years old. The bully was a stocky girl called Anna with bright red hair. She used to sit behind me in class and delighted in tying the bows of my pigtails together around the bar on the back of my chair. Of course, when I tried to stand up at the end of a lesson the chair would tip up with a clatter.

We were not allowed to tell tales in class, but when the teacher did eventually get annoyed about this daily occurrence, Anna changed her tactics and used to bully me in the playground instead. She would drag me by my plaits to the nearest fence and tie my hair together through the slats.

On one occasion, walking home from school at dinner time, she grabbed me and tied me to some iron railings outside a factory. I stood there for what seemed like hours crying until a lady came along and undid the knots in my ribbons.

I eventually retaliated in a way I feel ashamed about, but my options were limited. Anna was stronger than me and a confident fibber and, at that time, parents would not complain about bullying at school, even if they believed you. I took matters into my own hands by stealing her prized fountain pen and putting it down a drain on my way home from school. She was really distressed about the loss of the pen. I think she was the only child in school to have a fountain pen, bought for her by her overindulgent parents. Although she couldn't have known I had taken the pen, the bullying did stop, but I had no sense of satisfaction about what I had done.

The assembly hall loomed very large in our lives and was used for every purpose imaginable. After the register, each class assembled in the hall, starting with the little ones at the front and the biggest at the back. Our teachers sat around the edges and kept a very watchful eye on us for fidgeting or talking. Crippled children, of which there were many in those days, sat on little chairs by the teachers. Our head teacher, Mr Thompson, stood at the front and took the daily assembly. We always started with a hymn such as 'Morning Has Broken', 'Onward, Christian Soldiers', 'There is a Green Hill Far Away', 'Away in a Manger' – chosen according to the season of the year. After the hymn we had announcements about team results, school discipline, leavers and suchlike. We always finished with the Lord's Prayer.

Occasionally we had missionaries to talk to us in assembly about children who were worse off than we were – and some of the children in our school were very poor indeed. One lady who came regularly to see us was Miss Fry, who was connected with Fry's chocolate. She didn't ask for money but used to talk to us about being good and following God's teaching. At the end of her talk she would give every child in the school a little card with a beautifully decorated religious text on it.

Another way we were persuaded by missionaries to support less fortunate children was with a little booklet called *Sunny Smiles*. It was a tiny booklet about two inches square containing twenty or so monochrome photographs of young children – some black-skinned, some white. We had to sell these pictures to family and friends for a penny each. We tried hard to sell them, but even that small amount of money was hard to come by; one of our modern pennies is worth two and a half of those old pennies.

We always had a large number of children in school who had literally nothing and who always looked thin and hungry. Mom worried herself to death about one little girl called Janet. She would come to school in the coldest of winters with no socks, gloves or hat, and a threadbare coat. She always had nits and ringworm. It was difficult to give things to people, too, because it was a matter of considerable pride in those days to manage and not admit you needed a helping hand. However, Mom did somehow succeed in giving this little girl a warm cardigan and some socks. After she collapsed one day at school, an arrangement was made for her to receive a free dinner every day.

At certain times during the year we had a large contingent of gypsy children in school. The fair used to set up opposite the school on wasteland where the One Stop Shopping Centre in Perry Barr now stands. The Education Department had a duty to provide schooling for these children, so they joined our school for a few weeks each year. I think we were both fascinated and scared by them. The children were very ragged and not too clean, but certainly very quick-witted and confident, with wonderful tales to tell about their Romany lifestyle.

The hall was used daily by different classes in turn to do either gym (known as PE) or dancing (Movement and Music). We didn't have any gym equipment, and the lesson consisted of bending and stretching, touching toes, running round the hall in a circle, doing handstands and gambols. In dancing we had a teacher playing the piano and we had to pretend to be various things, for example, leaves blowing about on a windy day, a cat creeping through grass, thunder and lightning, an elephant swinging his trunk and so on. The dancing I enjoyed, the gym I hated – I still can't do gambols.

A feeling of terror swept over the school when we knew the nurses had arrived in the hall for their regular inspection of all the children. The hall even smelled different, with the all-pervading odour of Dettol, iodine, gentian violet and TCP. Nurses set up their tables in the four corners of the hall, and the teachers brought in each class in turn. We had to strip down to our knickers and vest. This alone was often very embarrassing, because most of us had holes in both garments and often the elastic would have gone in our knickers, which then had to be held up with safety pins. People only changed their underwear once a week, usually on a Sunday, so if the nurse came to school on Friday there would be some very grey and smelly-looking underwear.

Each child was brought trembling to the nurse who proceeded to inspect hair for nits, check all over your body for ringworm and look in your ears, fingernails and toenails for dirt. If they found a serious case of nits, out came the big scissors and your hair was cut off there and then. If you had ringworm in your head, your hair was shaved and your scalp covered with gentian violet, as were any worms found on your arms and legs. Gentian violet was a dye used as an antiseptic. It really was the brightest and most vivid violet colour imaginable.

You simply couldn't hide or disguise the great patches that these insensitive nurses daubed on arms, faces and heads. Your shame was very, very visible…

Notes went home to parents about further treatment and exclusion from school if the problem was not eradicated. Parents docilely accepted and supported this course of action; today I expect they would be shouting abuse.

We also had our teeth inspected in the hall by the dentist from the school clinic. This was the most barbaric experience imaginable, and it is no wonder that so many of my generation fear the dentist. Our teeth were not good anyway. Our diet during the war years and well into the fifties was limited, and dental hygiene wasn't taught or thought important. I think my sisters and I shared a toothbrush and we certainly didn't have toothpaste. Sometimes we dipped our brush in a little bit of salt to clean our teeth and at other times we rubbed our brush in the soot made from the residue from coal in our open fire. Cleaning teeth certainly wasn't a daily event; I think we cleaned our teeth for special occasions such as going to Sunday school or to the doctor's. Therefore when our annual school inspection came around nearly all of us were given a card to go to the dental clinic.

The atmosphere of the place was very frightening, with peculiar smells of gas and blood and disinfectant; huge black leather chairs and trays of metal instruments; children crying and clinging to their mothers; and others with bloodstained rags pressed to their mouths. There was a long production line of kiddies being dealt with; the dentist looked roughly into your mouth, gave either gas for lots of extractions, or cocaine for just one. (With cocaine, you were awake and could actually hear your tooth crunching as it was pulled out, as well as watch the dentist's contorted face as he exerted pressure on a stubborn tooth.)

Immediately after the extraction you were rushed into another room containing a row of small chairs in front of a trough through which water was running. You had to sit in front of this trough with a glass of water and spit the blood from your mouth into the trough. Because about ten children sat down at a time you had to watch everyone else's blood coming past you in the communal trough. I feel ill recording this, even though fifty years have passed! Once again, our parents didn't protest; in those days they seemed to accept that anything authority figures such as doctors, dentists or teachers decreed should go ahead unopposed.

Finally, the hall was used to perform our Christmas plays. This was quite a highlight in the school year and looked forward to by everyone. Teachers tended to keep the content of their chosen play secret from other classes to make the event more exciting. I remember one year when Linda and I were rehearsing our parts at home. She was in a higher class than me and so had a bigger part, but as she was practising her lines I realised that she was saying exactly the same lines as someone in my class. We compared notes and found both our classes were doing the same play.

There was much consternation when we told our teachers this next day. As Linda's class was older they had to learn a new play, and my class stuck to the original. I felt very important because I had discovered the duplication.

I remember only one teacher at Birchfield Road with great clarity. Her name was Miss Casey and I really loved her. To me she seemed old, but I expect she was in her early twenties. She wore the most beautiful clothes, some of which I remember clearly. She had a really lovely red dress with white spots, a scooped neckline, fitted waist and full skirt. It was made of good, heavy linen.

Miss Casey also had two princess-line coats, one maroon, one green, made fashionable by Princess Margaret in the early fifties. Dior introduced this style for his New Look collection after the war when, at last, clothes could be made extravagantly by using more material than was absolutely necessary. Each of the coats had a small velvet collar; they were fitted at the waist and then flared out into a full panelled skirt with a longer, more flattering hemline. Miss Casey wore smart, high-heeled lace-up shoes – a style I never saw on anyone else. She had pretty gold-rimmed glasses and short, strawberry-coloured hair.

But, more importantly, Miss Casey inspired me to learn; she

was always full of encouragement and enthusiasm, and was strict but fair. You always knew exactly where you were with her. She never raised her voice, but managed to maintain complete discipline in her class.

Our day started with multiplication tables, even though we were now at the top of the school and working towards grammar or secondary modern school entrance. Government strategy in 1952 meant there were two streams of senior schooling – grammar for academic skills and secondary modern for practical. We had to chant all our tables each day in a sing-song fashion – one two is two, two twos are four, three twos are six right through to one twelve is twelve, two twelves are twenty-four, and so on.

We had to practise our handwriting, too, and filled many pages joining whole rows of 'a's, 'b's and 'c's together. The style of writing the school followed was called Marion Richardson. There was always great emphasis on our work being both neat and accurate.

We had ten words a day to learn, both to spell and to understand. The list of words was put on the blackboard daily and we had to use our dictionaries to look up the meaning. We had to take a copy of the list home each night.

The following day Miss Casey would choose a pupil at random to stand by the cupboard at the side of the blackboard to spell out the words in turn. She would read the first word off the list on the board and you would have to spell it with the whole class watching the board to see if you got it right.

So that you couldn't see the word out of the corner of your eye, Miss Casey opened the cupboard door as a shield, so you were virtually standing in the cupboard to do your spelling test. Somehow the way she organised this didn't make any of us feel nervous or intimidated, and we felt extremely proud if we got all our words right. I rarely struggle with the spelling of a word and I am sure that is because of Miss Casey, her tests and her clever spelling rules, such as 'i' before 'e' except after 'c'.

And Miss Casey was certainly the prime mover in encouraging my love of books and reading. Every school day for the last fifteen minutes before the home time bell, she would sit up on her desk at the front of the class and read to us. The whole class could read really well by this time, but she understood perfectly the joy of being read to. She always chose a book with many chapters and an ongoing, exciting story and we would all look forward with great anticipation to each instalment. She introduced us to the Famous Five, *Huckleberry Finn*, *Tom Brown's Schooldays*, *Little Women*, *Black Beauty*, and so many stories and authors.

Towards the end of my years at Birchfield Road, and whilst in Miss Casey's class, we had a teacher trainee start called Mr Watson. He was young and good-looking and was to be placed in our class. I was probably about ten at this time and not very aware of relationships, but I can remember very clearly the look that passed between Miss Casey and Mr Watson when the head teacher first brought him into our room. It was magnetic. I am sure they behaved very discreetly at school, but we all knew they loved each other and very, very soon they were married.

I was sorry to leave Birchfield Road because I had mostly good experiences there. I had made friends and really enjoyed being in Miss Casey's class for two or three years. She encouraged us to go on and do our very best in our future schools. Nearly all the pupils in her class went on to grammar school, and that was a huge achievement for her as well as for us. I think teachers today would be staggered to learn that she had forty-nine pupils in her class.

In 1952, during summer tests, out of those forty-nine I came sixteenth with a total of 235 marks out of a possible 280. Miss Casey commented on my report, 'This is a rather disappointing result, Muriel must work much harder next year, she has the ability, but is a bit inclined to daydream.' She never let us rest on our laurels, but wanted us to strive for perfection and to appreciate the joy of learning. Her voice in my head still encourages me to persevere and to learn.

I am proud to say that my daughter is out of the same mould as 'my Miss Casey'. Maria has taught for many years at Prince Albert School in Aston, and is much loved by children and parents alike for her innovative and caring style of teaching.

Saturday Shopping with the Cowhide Bag

For many years Dad was a 'weekend father'. He worked for British Timken, an engineering company that made bearings for trains. His skill took him to Germany and Italy to do engineering work on railway systems that had been decimated by war. Mom has some wonderful photographs of Dad working on steam trains – many of the photographs show the devastation caused by British bombing.

To us, though, it seemed like a prolongation of the war. Dad had been missing in Italy during our early years and now he was permanently absent in Germany helping to put the pieces back together. I imagine we found it strange when Dad eventually became a full-time parent, and I think Mom was somewhat resentful of having her 'head of the household' hat removed after so many years managing alone.

The weekends, therefore, were very special, and we had lots of treats. We always had a car of some sort and spent many weekends in Wales, riding on the little steam train at Fairbourne, skimming stones on reservoirs, having picnics, climbing Dinas Mawddwy in an old Austin Seven and boiling up on the way. Petrol was still very scarce and strictly rationed, so a regular feature of our Saturday mornings was a trip to a garage at Villa Cross where the petrol coupons and money were exchanged for our weekly quota.

When the car had been fuelled up we used to visit Aunt Lil, Uncle Percy and cousin Pamela who, at that time, lived in Carpenters Road, Lozells. They lived in a row of terraced houses, all of which were kept immaculate by their owners. The steps were scrubbed and the pavements swept every day. Aunt Lil always had home-made cakes for us to eat, as well as ginger beer to drink. On the floor, in front of the coal fire, Aunt Lil had a rag rug that had been made by cutting old coats, trousers and skirts into strips. The strips were then carefully threaded through a hessian sack. Most people had such a rug in those days.

Every few weeks, whilst visiting Aunt Lil, we were shepherded into the garden to have our hair cut. Aunt Lil couldn't stand any sort of mess in the house so the job had to be done outside. They must have felt Dad was the most artistic so he did the actual cutting. We each sat on a high stool in turn with an old towel round our shoulders. The scissors Dad used to cut our hair with were the same ones used to trim wallpaper! They were always called 'the big scissors' – and they were big – the blades being about twelve inches long. You can imagine that it was a bit tricky to manoeuvre them around our small ears and fidgety heads. On one occasion Linda moved at a very delicate moment and Dad cut her ear, which bled most profusely. She screamed and shouted, but Dad just said, 'Never mind, ears heal easy.' It got to be quite a saying in the family and Linda and I still use it now when accidents happen and blood is spilled.

On the way home we got our sweetie ration. Once again, the coupons had to be passed over the counter, and a very few sweets were given in exchange. We had a glass jam jar each to put our sweets in when we got home. Linda always used to finish hers first and would be hankering after mine. I used to put my jar on the top of the wardrobe in an effort to prevent her from having them. It didn't work, though!

We lived a fairly free and easy life from Monday to Friday lunchtime, but Friday afternoons were awful. Mom started at the top of the house with a mad flurry of cleaning and tidying up before Dad came home. Her idea of tidying up was to open the nearest cupboard, stuff as many things as she could inside, and shut the door quickly. Dad used to go mad because every time he opened a door everything would come tumbling out.

Mom would work her way steadily through the bedrooms and bathroom and then down the stairs and into the hall. The hall was not carpeted and she hated polishing, so it was a regular thing for us girls to tie dusters to our feet and skate up and down the hall to give it a bit of a shine. By the time Dad got home on Friday evening I think Mom was too exhausted to enjoy seeing him. Of course, at the weekend she had to get all his shirts and under-clothes ready for the next trip on Monday morning. It must have been a difficult life for both of them.

As we grew older and Dad returned home for good there seemed to be more and more chores to be done. We always argued over who would do the washing-up, the ironing, the dusting and the shopping. Dad got really fed up with the bickering. Withholding our pocket money hadn't worked so he came up with a brilliant plan.

He drew up a 'Chores Chart' and stuck it on the living room wall for all to see. Along the top were the jobs that had to be done and along the side the names of each of us girls. There was no obligation on any of us to do any particular job on a specific day, but every time we completed a task we could put a tick in the appropriate column against our name. At the end of a week it showed very clearly who was pulling their weight and who wasn't. It also showed our different approaches. I always tried to do one job on the list each day, and so did Lorna. Linda went on for as long as possible without doing anything at all and then found she was grounded for a week whilst she caught up with the rest of us. It was a hard lesson at the time, but one that has stood me in good stead throughout life.

We used to have a lot of tradesmen calling at the house in those days. The ones that I can remember are milkman, baker, laundry man, coalman, knife sharpener, grocer, window cleaner, chimney sweep, insurance man and pop man. We also had visits from quite a few tramps, or 'men of the road' as they were called, as well as the rag-and-bone man.

The rag and bone man would make a present of a goldfish in a glass bowl to householders if he was given a decent amount of rags – or bones off the meat! The bones were collected and used in the manufacture of china – hence the term 'bone china'. I don't know what he did with the old rags; sometimes I felt we were already wearing them as all our clothes and shoes were second, third or even fourth hand-me-downs.

The milkman, baker and coalman all came in a cart drawn by a horse and we were honour bound by Dad to follow the horses with a bucket and shovel to the end of our lane. If the horse dropped any manure we had to collect it for the garden. We always hoped the horses would go beyond the end of the lane before dropping their huge steaming dollops, thereby letting us off the hook.

The insurance man was really strange and always asked to go to the bathroom every time he came. Mom was quite suspicious about him but it was ages before she realised that he was taking things from the airing cupboard. Mom stored the spare toilet rolls, soap and, more worryingly, our pants and vests in there, and he helped himself to all of them.

The laundry man was fascinating too. He would arrive with a brown paper parcel tied up with string, and a book listing the many items the laundry handled. We had to tick what had been sent the previous week and check that it had all come back: white tablecloths, sheets, towels, shirts, separate shirt collars, chair backs and arm covers – all starched and stiff like boards. Then off he would go with the current week's parcel and his newly ticked book. The brown paper and string had to be saved from week to week; they were precious commodities then.

The milkman was from the Co-op and when he came to the door for his money we had to give him our number, which I still remember – 255816. Every Christmas, Mom would go up to the Co-op head office in High Street, Birmingham to collect her 'divi' (dividend/share). I don't know how much she got, but I expect it helped with the Christmas festivities.

The grocer, too, was always greeted with great excitement. He had been our grocer for years, even before we moved to Aldridge Road. Linda and I used to take Mom's order book into the shop on Thursday morning and the grocer would get it ready and packed up in a sturdy box for delivery on Friday afternoon. He marked the prices down in the book at the side of each item. Often, if he had a new line in bacon or cheese, he would send little samples to be tried. This was the bit we looked forward to and, as the rationing restrictions were slowly lifted, we occasionally got samples of jam or biscuits to try. It was wonderful. We had to save all the bags from the sugar, currants, raisins, rice and dried goods to be returned the following week for refilling. The bags were made of strong, blue paper and had to be looked after carefully. Butter, cheese and bacon were wrapped in squares of greaseproof paper, and salt came in a big solid block which Mom had to grind down on a metal grater.

Fresh food had to be fetched on a Saturday by Linda and me

from Perry Barr. On a hook in the pantry hung the cowhide bag. This bag was made from the skin of a cow and was formed, not as usual with the leather side outward, but showing the real furry skin. It was a bright chestnut colour with white markings, and you could almost see a lovely coloured cow munching grass in a field! It makes me cringe now, but it was part of the ritual of fetching the Sunday joint, fresh vegetables and fruit for the weekend.

Linda and I knew the list of things we had to buy almost by heart. We were given a £1 note and threatened with punishment worse than death if we lost it. First we had to go to the butcher's to fetch a whole leg of lamb costing not more than 17/6 (about 87p) – and a few 'lights' for the cat. These were disgusting, being the innards of all sorts of animals, and given for a few pence. There was no tinned cat food then. The butcher used to wrap the lights up in many layers of newspaper so that the blood would not drip through.

Next we had to go to the greengrocer's with the remaining 2/6 (about 13p) to buy enough fruit and vegetables for a family of six for a week! As I remember, we got potatoes, cabbage, carrots, sprouts (if in season) and some bananas and oranges, and occasionally a coconut. Apples, pears, damsons and soft fruits came from the garden at home or from relatives, and the vegetables were supplemented by those grown at home – lots of beans, peas, onions and potatoes – until they ran out.

Linda and I would waltz along swinging the bag between us. I think we always enjoyed going to Perry Barr – it was a little village in 1950, with lots of interesting shops and no dangerous traffic. There was the library and the dolls' hospital and Grandma Rose's chapel, cake shops and sweet shops, and the Rose and Crown where Mom and Dad had their wedding reception, the speedway track and the greyhound racing track, the fire station and Harris the cleaners, with its beautiful gardens. We would linger for ages looking in all the windows, as well as stopping to chat with any friends we met along the way.

Sometimes, if we were lucky, the greengrocer would give us a pair of feet cut from the chickens he sold in his shop. The feet often had the sinews left in them and we considered it great fun to pull them up making the feet curl as though they were still alive. What horrors we were!

The cowhide bag had a life apart from shopping, and sometimes made a much more glamorous outing. For example, in 1953 we – and the bag – went to London to see how the city had been decorated for the Queen's Coronation. The decorations were magnificent. The streets were still lined with rows and rows of tiered seating made from scaffolding and wooden planks, on which people had sat and waited for many days and nights to watch the young Queen's procession from Buckingham Palace to Westminster Abbey.

The bag came with us everywhere and we have a lovely photograph of me, Linda, Lorna and Daddy – and the bag – promenading along the seafront in Wales. I wonder what we carried in the bag that day. Was it spare nappies for the baby, Jennifer? Was it Mom's purse? A hanky? A hairbrush? A camera? A picnic? Who knows what?

I feel sad that I don't know what happened to the cowhide bag, because it was as much a part of my life for many years as going to school, getting washed – or Christmas.

The Games we Played and the Trolleys we Made

We had so little when we were growing up, and yet I can vividly remember busy, sun-filled days when bedtime always came too soon. We had very, very few shop-bought toys to amuse us but we were never bored or still.

The first real games that I can remember centre on the garden at Livingstone Road. There was a large horde of small children – me, my cousins and sisters, and friends who lived in the road – and we gathered daily in the garden. Most of our early games involved riding little trikes round and round the long earthen paths, or playing with our dolls and teddies.

We didn't have cots or pushchairs and prams for our dolls, as children do now, but we made do with cardboard boxes from the shoe shop. Somehow, in our eyes, these became the most fantastic cots, with a bit of old towel as a blanket, or prams with a piece of string attached to pull them along. Children at that time must have driven shopkeepers mad, because it was a regular occupation for youngsters to go around to all the shops asking for boxes.

A large part of our early years' play revolved around 'making tents'. Everybody had a wooden clothes horse to dry the washing inside on wet days; some horses had two sides and some had three. We used to drag both Mom's and Aunt Doll's clothes horse along the hall, down the steep back step and into the garden. We would prop the 'horses' up as best we could, then drape them all over with the itchy grey blankets from Uncle Frank's removal lorry. The blankets were normally used to protect furniture from scratches during transit.

It is hard to describe the enchantment of this game. We really felt that we were in a dark and secret world, and believed that the grown-ups couldn't see or hear us. I can still remember the sort of murky half-light that we sat in. Sometimes we played at house and sometimes we played cowboys and Indians, and sometimes we did nothing at all – just sat pulling up tufts of grass or letting the dirt and stones trickle through our fingers whilst we talked of all the daring things we would do.

Another favourite game was skipping. There was a lovely big yard at Livingstone Road made out of strong blue bricks with a diamond pattern etched into them. The washing mangle stood on this yard, and at the side of the yard were the coal sheds and the outside toilet. But we used the remainder of the yard for skipping. We ached for one of the attractive skipping ropes you could get then; they had lovely wooden painted and varnished handles with ball bearings in them, and just the right length and weight of thick white rope. However, we had to make do with the washing line folded three or four times to get the right length. We got quite tangled up in the rope as we tried to skip; the strands would keep separating and getting caught round the buckles on our sandals. Sometimes Aunt Doll and Mom would come out to hold one end of the line each. They would turn the rope so that several children could skip together in a long line, singing, 'All in together, girls! Never mind the weather, girls!'

Another skipping memory is connected with a poorly young girl from next door whose name was Mary. She was completely paralysed, and spent all her days lying on a bed with cot sides. In cold or wet weather the bed was wheeled in front of the big picture window at the front of the house so that Mary could see the people passing in the road. On fine days the bed was wheeled outside into the garden at the back of the house. We used to climb up and look over the wall at Mary and try to talk to her, but sadly she couldn't understand or reply. The kind folk who looked after her tried very hard to make her life as good as possible, and always had a birthday party for Mary. Of course, we knew of her disabilities and so appropriate presents were bought; but others who were invited from the local school did not know Mary and on one occasion a young child bought her one of those very skipping ropes we so much coveted. To our shame we were jealous of Mary being given such a rope, but Mom and Aunt Doll cried for the pity of it. They loved Mary very much.

As we got a little older, and whilst still living at Livingstone Road, our horizons became wider. There wasn't the same worry then about letting young children out to play alone. We always felt quite safe and could wander at will around the local streets. We had a square in which we were allowed to play. The square consisted roughly of Livingstone Road, Putney Road, Hutton Road, Westminster Road, and Havelock Road in Handsworth, Birmingham. We wandered for hours up and down these roads; there was very little traffic to worry us, and we ran back and forth across the roads without a care in the world. We played simple games such as tig, and blind man's buff, or we tied a piece of rope to the crossbar of a lamp post to make a swing. We played whip and top and jacks and fivestones for endless hours, sitting on the edge of the gutter in the dust and the dirt. We begged or borrowed a small piece of chalk to make hopscotch on the pavement. If we couldn't get chalk we would spend forever looking for just the sort of stone you were able to draw with. This would be either soft red sandstone or limestone.

On high days and holidays we were given a halfpenny and allowed to go to Stoats' sweet shop at the top of Putney Road; the very limit of our territory. Of course, we had to have a sweet ration coupon, too. Stoats was absolutely magical. There were rows and rows of delicious looking sweets on every shelf in tall glass jars. The shopkeeper would take down the jar of our choice and gently tip 2 oz into his weighing scales. Next, the sweets were tipped into a small, triangular shaped white paper bag with a serrated top, before being passed to us.

Besides the sweets in jars there were other lovely things to choose from the well-stocked ledges arranged like tiered seating at a sports stadium. These ran all along the front of the counter. There were gobstopper balls, which changed colour as you sucked them. They usually started a bright yellow or orange and changed through the whole spectrum of colours, taking about an hour to suck all the way to the middle, where there was often a tiny seed or nut. We could get liquorice root, which looked just like a twig off a tree, and really had rather a peculiar taste, but it lasted for hours and hours.

When you tired of chewing it you put it in your pocket. Hours later it would be brought out again covered in bits of dust and fluff and put straight back into your mouth for another good chew. We also had black imps, which were minute little black dots of sweets and tasted very hot. These were sold in small, square metal tins with a tiny hole in one corner, which released the 'imps' one at a time. Cherry lips were also tiny, bright red, and shaped like miniature quarter moons – you got hundreds of those to the ounce.

We had bags of sherbet crystals (known as kali). You had to lick your finger, dip it into the bag and then into your mouth to suck off the sharp, sugary crystals. At the end of the day, many children were walking round with bright orange fingers from the sherbet. If you were really friendly with someone you demonstrated your friendship by saying, 'Want a dip?' Hygiene was a stranger to us.

We were also allowed, because it was part of our square, to go into the 'gilly gardens'. These were allotments beginning on the opposite side of Livingstone Road from our house and stretching all the way over to Wellington Road. We were allowed to walk the black cinder paths of the gilly gardens to the very perimeter – but definitely not beyond. Wellington Road carried a lot of traffic even in those days.

The allotments were called the gilly gardens locally because every plot holder grew the most colourful and fragrant wallflowers (gilliflowers) in the spring. The clove-like perfume of the flowers filled the air and I was always tempted to touch the pretty, velvety petals of the wallflowers. I love growing wallflowers, and when they bloom I am carried back to those days. How we relished dragging our feet along the paths, making little clouds of dust, collecting stones and sticks and looking for caterpillars. The ones we found were big, fat and multicoloured, with hundreds of little hairs protruding from them. Those seen today seem very unexciting. We used to put them in jam jars with a cabbage leaf, believing that they would turn into butterflies.

There were many, many butterflies then, of every size and colour, and the gilly gardens was the best place to see large numbers all together. We used to go home from our walks tired and dishevelled; I can still remember how my feet looked with lots of fine dust between my toes. We didn't wear socks except for Sunday school and often our sandals had worn out soles, which had been repaired with cornflake packets. Dad used to cut round the shape of our shoes and then insert the cards inside our shoes so they would last a bit longer.

An abrupt end came to these carefree days when we moved into my Grandma's house in Aldridge Road. There were many new ways of life to learn. We had to change school, so we lost many of our little friends and, for the first time in our young lives, we were not living with cousins and aunts and uncles. The road we now lived on was much busier, and strange to us, so Mom was not so keen for us to venture outside.

We did have a big garden but it did not have the mystery of the previous one. There were no high walls to peer over, no secret places to hide, no trees to climb and no sense of adventure. We did adjust to it of course, but not without pain. I missed my cousin, Margaret, quite dreadfully and often went back to stay at Aunt Doll's so we could be together.

As my younger sister, Lorna, got bigger she became a companion to me and filled the gap left by Margaret. We played together much more than Linda and I had ever done. The games we played at Aldridge Road were, at first, simple and confined to the house and garden.

We had a lovely little wooden house of our own at the end of the garden, and many of our games were played in there. We had a big see-saw, too, and a swing, and spent many happy hours playing on them. As all other children did in those times we occupied ourselves by playing marbles. Besides lovely coloured cat's eye marbles, milky marbles, tiger's eyes and gobbies, we had bags and bags of shiny silver ball bearings, which Dad got from British Timken. There was quite a cut-throat trade in 'marlies' between children, and there was some strict order of preference and value, which now escapes me. The trading of marbles could take equally as long as the game and certainly caused more argument.

We played many different ball games such as pig in the middle, and another, more complicated game, whereby you threw the ball against the wall, but when it bounced back you didn't catch it but the person behind you did as you ran to the back of the queue. You had to keep going with this until the ball was dropped or missed. There were many bumps and bangs as everyone jostled for position.

As we got a little older and started to go to school on our own, Mom relented and let us start playing 'out the front'. Just down the road was, and still is, a most famous zigzag bridge, which crossed the River Tame. In fact, there are two bridges side by side. When the replacement road was built with its new bridge, there was a fierce campaign to save part of the old road and bridge because of its historical interest. We used to go down to play on the old bridge and loved walking along its walls and hiding in the cut-outs, which were originally used for people to stand in whilst horse-drawn carriages passed by.

As we got bigger, another amusement was to feed the pigs. Behind our house in Aldridge Road was a big allotment, and beyond that was a pig farm. During the war, and for some time afterwards, people were encouraged to keep pigs, and everybody had to save scraps for them to eat. Mom used to save our scraps in a white enamel bucket; they smelled and looked absolutely foul and were called 'swill'. Every few days Lorna and I would set off with the bucket between us for the long walk to the pig farm. We used to walk down Aldridge Road and turn right into a rough lane covered in black ash, which bordered the side of the allotment.

Eventually we came to another right turn, and this led to the pigs. Because I was slightly taller than Lorna, the bucket always tilted to her side and the slops came over the top and down her legs, but strangely I don't remember her being upset by it. When we arrived at the pigs we didn't have to see anybody but simply found an empty trough and tipped the 'swill' in. The pigs would come running like mad. I liked the pigs very much, especially the babies, but I didn't like the smell of them or the look of their food; it made me feel quite sick. To this day I cannot bear to use the word 'swill', and when someone says they are going to 'swill their hands' or 'swill out a few clothes', you can imagine the picture in my mind!

Like most children of that time, we were forever trying to make trolleys. These consisted of an orange box, a long piece of wood, two small wheels at the front, two pram wheels at the back and a stout piece of rope for the steering. Collecting the equipment together and making the trolley could take the whole of the six-week summer holiday from school.

Things were not thrown away with such easy abandon in those hard times, and it could take such a long time to find the wheels or cadge an orange box from the greengrocer. And the mechanics of it all for two small girls was quite difficult, too. However, we managed to make some fairly decent trolleys and proudly trundled them up and down the footpath for hours on end. We were fairly sedate with ours, but you often saw boys with really sophisticated affairs. They would have frantic races with one another until most had crashes or the wheels fell off, necessitating hasty rebuilds before the next day's sport. But that was all part of the fun.

As time went on we wandered further and further away. Eventually Mom allowed us to go about half a mile down Aldridge Road to Perry Barr Park. It was a lovely place, with shallow streams in which to catch tiddlers, swings and round-abouts and witch's hats, and lots of winding paths to explore with colourful flower beds on either side. There was a big lake in one part of the park with a fast-flowing weir. We used to climb up onto the wall so that we could watch how fast the water was going and what debris had been caught in the grill at the bottom of the weir. I shudder to think now of the dangers we were in. Mom and Dad were caring and careful parents, and yet they let us do all this exploring alone.

Catching tiddlers was a favourite pastime and one that lasted all day. We would set off early for the half-mile walk to the park with a garden cane and a bit of an old stocking fixed on the end for a fishing net. We carried a jam jar with a string tied round the neck to put the tiddlers in. Mom would give us a piece of bread smeared with treacle for our dinner and a sterilised milk bottle full of cold tea with a screw of greased paper in the top to prevent spillage. Watches were a luxury, so unless we saw the park keeper and could ask, we never knew the time to go home until it became dusk. Again, and in the light of today's climate, I marvel at what now seems to have been a most casual attitude on Mom's part towards our safety.

Mom was brought up sharply – and shockingly – in the end.

Lorna and I still went to Brownies at the church at the top of Livingstone Road. We used to take a short bus ride from Aldridge Road to the Odeon in Perry Barr where we got off the bus, crossed the road and walked up Livingstone Road, calling at Aunt Doll's to collect Margaret on the way. From there we dawdled together to the church. The return journey was the same in reverse.

One night Lorna and I were almost back to the end of Livingstone Road, walking along holding hands. Suddenly a man came alongside on a pushbike. He grabbed Lorna in his arms and started to ride off with her. I knew I was supposed to scream and shout, but not a sound would come out of my mouth. I don't know where I found the courage or the strength, but I ran after him and grabbed Lorna's leg and pulled and pulled with all my might. It caused his bike to wobble dreadfully and he cursed and shouted at me but I wouldn't let go. He had to drop Lorna in the end and we made the rest of the way home, shaking and crying. Mom got the police straight away but the man was never found. This, of course, was the end of our unaccompanied roaming, and our first experience of the real world.

Confined to the house and garden, Lorna and I found a new way of amusing ourselves. We decided to start a club, which was secret because its purpose was to find ways of getting everybody in the family a Christmas present. We thought we would either make presents or save our pocket money to buy them. On winter days we used to shut ourselves in our tiny bedroom and sit for hours at the dressing table, which we used as a desk. We had little booklets of paper and pens and anything else we could find to make us look important and efficient. We thought we were really clever devising a name for the club, which no one else would understand. We called the club *Serpent Bulc*, which, as you may realise, is a rearrangement of the letters *Present Club*. Although this secret scheming and planning kept us occupied for many weeks, I don't actually remember us either buying or making any presents for anyone... but how we enjoyed it all.

In the summer, we tried to find ways to amuse ourselves in the garden. I often used to gather together my doll's clothes (of which I had many) and set about doing my laundry. I used to get a bowl of water from the house and a small piece of green soap, which was so worn down that you could almost see through it. Nothing was wasted then, and there was no washing powder to speak of – or washing-up liquid. Mom used to save all the little pieces of leftover soap, put them into an old stocking, and then soften the enclosed bits in a little warm water. The mixture was then squeezed firmly together to make a new bar of soap.

I did my washing as taught by Mom. Clothes were immersed, one at a time, in the water and the dirtiest parts, usually collars and cuffs, were rubbed on a wooden board with the soap; sometimes very dirty marks had to be scrubbed with a brush. As each item was washed it was set aside for rinsing. Mom always did three rinses, changing the water each time. In the last rinse she (and I) put a 'blue bag' to improve the look of the washing. When I was young everybody used blue bags.

Reckitt's blue bags were small, bright blue blocks of compacted powder, wrapped in a fine linen bag. They were swished about in the final rinse water until they dissolved a little; the clothes were then immersed. You would think that dipping soft white nappies into such brilliantly blue water would stain them, but it did not; it simply made them glow whiter – or so the advertising slogans said.

When I had finished this performance, I used to tie a piece of string to the shed at one end of the lawn and to the rose trellis at the other. Mom used to lend me her bag of pegs and I would hang out my baby's washing. It gave me a thrill to see all the tiny clothes along the line. I had exactly the same thrill the first time I hung Simon's nappies out. I do think modern parents miss something with their disposables. I never tired of seeing my children's nappies blowing in the wind on a sunny day.

Boredom often caused us to get into mischief, especially during the long holidays. Once, when cousin Margaret was staying with us, we decided to play a trick on Mom and Dad. At the time, we were all sleeping in 'the big bedroom' at Aldridge Road. Lorna, Linda and I slept together in a double bed, with Jennifer in her cot at the side of us. When Margaret stayed, she slept in the bed with us. It was not thought unusual – we kept each other warm. There was no central heating and, in the winter, the windows often had ice on the insides.

On the night in question, we went off to bed with instructions to behave ourselves and get off to sleep. Of course, we lay awake in bed, plotting mischief. We decided to get Jennifer out of her cot, gag her and put her underneath our bed. She made a fuss so we got underneath the bed with her. Then we had the idea of opening the window to make it look as though we had all run away. When Mom came up to check on us, she started screaming. I don't think I shall ever forget her shouting for Dad whilst leaning out of the window as far as she could, sobbing, 'Ken, Ken, come quickly! The kids have gone!'

We never imagined the shock we were going to give her – our world didn't include kidnapping or abductions, and we were oblivious to the fact that we might have suffocated Jennifer with the gag.

Other mischievous games had a lighter side. We used to love playing hide and seek, and most of the time it was harmless fun. However, on one occasion we got into a mess, even with that simple game. In the front bedroom there was a large oak wardrobe with a central door with a mirror. The wardrobe was made out of three sections. The base was in the form of a long drawer for blankets; the middle section was for hanging clothes; and finally there was a decorative cornice, which balanced on the top. Linda decided to hide in the clothes hanging section. However, she fidgeted so much that the middle part of the wardrobe toppled off the base and onto the bed that ran alongside it. Of course, this meant that the door was face down on the bed, with Linda trapped inside. None of us could lift the wardrobe back up onto the base and we thought Linda would suffocate. Mom had to get the neighbours to help her right the wardrobe to let Linda out.

As the years moved on we spent less and less time playing our childish games. We began to make friends as individuals outside the family. We no longer went around as the Bridgewater gang and the Sweetman gang. Instead we made friends with girls – and boys – from our schools and the youth club. But I feel our closeness as children was valuable; it taught us such a lot about loyalty, friendship and sharing. Even though we have followed many different directions, and we each have very different characters, when we are reunited we fall back into our childhood roles. We share the same sense of humour, shared thought processes, instant rapport... and we never need to finish a sentence!

Flying Off the Shed Roof

We moved to Aldridge Road soon after Jennifer was born in 1949 when I was about six years old. I can't recall being excited or any emotion at all, really, but it gradually dawned on us that Grandma Rose had died, that she wasn't coming back, that we were going to live in her house and that Linda and I were going to a different school.

The pull of our Livingstone Road roots was strong, and we often made the long walk back to Number 36. We still went to the Congregationalist Church on Westminster Road for Sunday school, Brownies, Junior Church and Guides.

We made a pilgrimage every Saturday morning to the Odeon cinema at Perry Barr. It cost 6d for a wonderful morning's entertainment. We saw Roy Rogers and *Zorro* and *Flash Gordon* and Charlie Chaplin and the wonders of 3D cinema when we were each given a pair of cardboard glasses with one red eyepiece and one green. We thrilled as the cowboys and Indians on their horses careered towards us. Small boys took their toy guns to the pictures with them and shot wildly at the Indians.

Margaret's eye trouble was worsened, I think, as a result of the Saturday morning pictures. We loved to sit near the front, despite being warned about it harming our eyes. One morning a film included shots of a big steam train coming towards us, and during this sequence something seemed to happen to Margaret's eyes. The pupils became detached and disappeared somewhere round the side of her head. For years and years Margaret had to wear glasses with one eyepiece at a time covered over with pink sticky plaster and had to endure operations on her eyes well into adulthood.

Despite the hankering to wander back, our base was now Aldridge Road. I can remember the house fairly well; nearly everything seemed to go on in the back room, which overlooked the garden. There was a front room but, as in most houses in those days, that was the 'best room' for important visitors only. It contained two comfortable armchairs, a dinner wagon, a china cabinet and a piano.

On special occasions, such as Christmas, we went into the front room to listen to Dad playing the piano. He was a good pianist and could play by ear as well as from sheet music. He had a repertoire of several different types of song. He used to sing and play many of Gracie Fields numbers, such as 'Sally, Sally, Pride of our Alley' and 'My Old Man said Follow the Van'. Two of my favourites were 'The Isle of Capri' – a rather wistful love song – and 'The Rich Maharajah of Magador – he had Ten Thousand Women and maybe more'. The Maharajah song had to be sung very loudly with the piano lid open and the hard pedal down.

Dad used to sit on the stool, well away from the piano, with his arms at full stretch and his head flung back for this performance. We all joined in the chorus, which went 'Aaaaaaaaaaaaaaaaaaaaaaaa' whilst Dad accompanied us with the Indian snake-charmer music.

Sometimes Dad played ragtime jazz in the style of Scott Joplin. He used to open the lid of the piano and put sheets of newspaper against the hammers to give the right effect. Dad had many 78 rpm records by the pianist Charlie Kunz that he loved to listen to on our wind-up gramophone. He preferred to be able to play the music of these artists accurately, so he used the sheet music that was kept in the piano stool. The music sheets had beautifully illustrated front covers and would be the equivalent of today's album covers. A sleeve of stiff brown paper protected precious volumes of music, and the edges of the music sheets, too, were bound in brown paper for easier turning over of the pages.

In the back room there was a dining table, chairs, sideboard, two well-worn armchairs, a fireplace and a radio. There was a big wooden overmantel surrounding the coal fire; it had a central mirror and a big high shelf on which stood two huge brown German jugs, one on either side of the clock. Birth, marriage and death certificates, medals, old coins, important letters and receipts were stored in the jugs for safe keeping.

The sideboard was typical 1930s – rather ugly and

cumbersome. It had the usual cupboards and drawers, as well as a mirror-lined central cupboard, grandly known as a 'cocktail cabinet'. It had two rather neat cubbyholes with lift-up lids on either side of the cocktail cabinet. The sideboard was supposed to hold crockery, cutlery and glasses – but not in our house!

The cocktail cabinet section housed the medicines, including poisons; the cubbyholes were home to our many gloves, hats and bus tokens (kept in a strong blue bag); the cupboards and drawers held a huge assortment of things which Mom couldn't find a place for anywhere else – knitting and sewing, old brown paper bags, tins of buttons, string, spare shirt collars, cookery books, a childcare manual of the 1930s called *The Motherhood Book* and – strangest of all – my two waist length plaits which had been cut off when I went to grammar school. These stayed in the cupboard, complete with ribbons, until mites got into the plaits and they had to be thrown away.

On the windowsill we had one of the very first mechanical pencil sharpeners. It nearly drove our neighbours mad trying to guess what the strange whirring noise could be as we sharpened our pencils! There were three holes of differing sizes in which to push our pencils, with a little drawer beneath to collect the many shavings. I loved those shavings – the curls of wood were beautiful and of many different colours – a reflection of the assortment of pencils sharpened.

Our meals were always taken around the table; there was no distraction from radio or television as we talked together. Sometimes Mom and Dad were sulking with one another and Mom would say, 'Linda, does your Dad want a cup of tea?' Then Dad would say, 'Linda, tell your mother, "Yes".' I can well remember the sort of sickly feeling I used to get when this was going on.

All our parties were held around the same table. We didn't have many chairs, so Dad used to bring in a big plank from the shed and stretch it between two chairs, allowing several small bottoms to sit side by side. I recall really disliking the itchy blanket that covered the plank.

For some reason the Christmas puddings were always made on the dining room table rather than in the kitchen. Mom used to scald the washing-up bowl for mixing, and we all helped weigh the fruit and chop up the peel and cherries. The breadcrumbs had to be made by rubbing stale bread through the metal colander – it made your fingers very sore. The almonds were skinned by dipping them in boiling water and squeezing the nuts between your fingers until they popped out of their skins. We all had a hand in the making, and we all had a final stir when we had to make a wish. I expect we wished for something special for Christmas, although I can't remember any of my wishes now.

Mom always wore an old stocking over her head when making the puddings, to prevent hairs from falling in. One memorable year Jennifer, who was quite small, came in with a stocking pulled over her head and well down over her eyes. Mom said there was no need to have it that far down but Jennifer immediately answered back with, 'What about my eyelashes?' It made us all laugh.

I remember, too, that Dad used to cover the table with an oiled protective cloth and newspaper in order to make wax brooches. I don't know whether this was purely a hobby or a moneymaking venture. We were never really well off. He used to have lots of different coloured strips of sealing wax, little pieces of shaped card, and gold safety pins for the fasteners. The wax was melted with a candle and dabbed onto the cards; by using two or three different colours, the most beautiful swirling patterns were made. The completed brooches were lovely... I wonder what happened to them all?

Upstairs there were three bedrooms and a bathroom. Initially, my sisters and I slept in the large back bedroom, and Mom and Dad in the front. The boxroom was used to store clutter. As we got bigger the clutter was cleared so that Lorna and I could share the boxroom. There was just enough room for a double bed, a dressing table and a built-in cupboard that Dad made. Mom and Dad moved into the back room and Linda and Jen shared the front.

It used to be bitterly cold in the bedrooms when we were small. There was no central heating, and often on winter mornings the inside of the windows would be covered in thick frost.

The patterns the frost made on the windows were beautiful, fern-like creations, lacy fairies' wings and delicate butterflies. You had to scratch the window with your fingernails to make a hole to look outside. Whenever we were poorly Mom used to carry a bucket of coal, wood and paper upstairs to light a fire in the grate. We had to be really ill for this to happen – it was a luxury that couldn't easily be afforded.

Often we dreaded going to bed in winter because the sheets were icy cold. I don't know why we didn't have hot-water bottles – maybe they were not generally available. We did have one stone hot-water bottle but this got cracked and couldn't be replaced. Dad came up with an ingenious idea for warming the beds. He acquired a metal drum into which he wired a light bulb; when the cable was plugged in, the bulb heated the drum and the drum heated the bed. Luxury!

We were supposed to switch 'the heater' off and put it onto the floor before we got into bed, but Linda and I very quickly discovered that if we put our heads under the covers, there was enough light coming from the bulb to read by.

We were often punished for this dangerous practice – the heater could have got too hot and set the bed on fire. Usually we were given the slipper. We had to bend over whilst Mom – or, more usually, Dad – whacked us on the bottom with a carpet slipper. Mom used to be really upset saying, through clenched teeth, 'God forgive me, but you deserve it.' There was much support for the maxim 'spare the rod and spoil the child' in those days.

Often when we had been naughty Dad used to twist our ear lobes between his thumb and finger whilst saying, 'Do you want a thick ear?' That really hurt too. But, worst of all, was the razor strop. This was a leather strap used for sharpening cut-throat razors. It hung on a hook by the pantry door, and if we even hinted that we were about to step out of line, Mom or Dad would say, 'Fetch the strap.' This had an instant effect; the strop was a very fearful weapon, made from a thick three-inch-wide leather belt with a heavy brass hook on each end. It was never used on any of us – the words 'fetch the strap' were deterrent enough.

The bathroom was thought to be very modern by the standards of the late 1940s and early 1950s. There was an inside toilet, a washbasin and a bath! We were one of the few families in the road to have a means of heating water for a bath without using the back boiler of the coal fire.

This meant we could have a bath with hot water in the summer when the fire wasn't normally alight. The reason for this was 'the geyser'. This was a huge cylindrical copper tank that stood at the end of the bath. It was filled with cold water by a system of pipes. Once the tank was full of water, a match was used to light the circular gas ring beneath it. When the water was boiling, a tap that protruded from halfway up the tank was turned on and hot water gushed out into the bath.

The whole family bathed in one tank of water; babies, followed by toddlers, followed by Mom, followed by Dad.

At the side of the house were the kitchen, the pantry and the coal shed. The kitchen was small, but a place of much activity. There was a sturdy pine chest of drawers along one wall, with a cooker beside it. The surface of the chest was used for cooking preparation, pastry rolling, serving out and so on. Of course there were no easy to clean surfaces, so the chest had to be scrubbed daily with a scrubbing brush to keep it fresh and germ-free. It had many score marks in its surface from knives, hot pans and kitchen implements. Strangely, the drawers of the chest were used to store cleaning materials, shoe polish, floor polish, dusters, blue bags, soap, and a whole lot of other household paraphernalia.

On the other wall of the kitchen was a sink with a wooden draining board, and next to this was a copper boiler that was lit early every Monday morning to do the most heavily soiled washing. During the week the boiler was covered with a wooden lid, enabling it to double as another working surface in the kitchen.

At the end of the kitchen was a pantry where quantities of crockery and food were stored. Along the back wall of the pantry were floor-to-ceiling shelves, where Mom piled our odd assortment of plates, dishes, cups, saucers, vegetable dishes, meat plates, saucepans, colanders, sieves and graters. At each side of the pantry there were two wide cold slabs. Many houses had cold slabs, as there were no refrigerators. Cold slabs were made from a two-inch thick piece of concrete or marble on which foodstuffs such as butter, milk and cheese were kept to preserve them.

Most people had meat safes, too. These were small metal cupboards with fine mesh doors in which meat was kept cool and protected from flies. People would put their Sunday joint in the safe, together with sausage, bacon and ham. This was really important; in my youth I often saw pieces of unprotected meat crawling with maggots because a blowfly had been allowed to land on it to lay its eggs.

The milk often turned sour in the summer months and, as nothing could be wasted, we used to make it into cream cheese. This was done by tipping the soured milk into a muslin bag, tying it up and leaving it hanging from the tap above the sink overnight. The watery substance would drip through the muslin leaving the cheesy curds in the bag. When it was thoroughly drained, Mom would mix the curd with a bit of salt and spread it on a chunk of bread for our tea.

The milk always went sour when there was a thunderstorm, too. To avoid waste and to soothe our fears Mom and Dad used to bring us downstairs into the kitchen, warm all the milk in a saucepan and allow us to drink it. Whenever I hear thunder now I remember those cosy times in the kitchen when my sisters and I sat in a row on the wooden chest drinking milk, and defying the thunder and lightning.

The garden was big and well kept. The kitchen was on the side of the house with a door leading down a steep step into the entry. The garden door from the living room was rarely used. In the first part of the garden there was a crazy paved yard (now it would be called a patio, I suppose). Immediately beyond this was a rockery about three yards square, but it was a most unusual rockery. Craftily, beneath it, my Grandad had built an air raid shelter. It was very sophisticated, consisting of a neat, square room with beds and storage cupboards, and was accessed by steps leading down from the yard. There were two six-inch diameter breathing shafts coming up to the surface, carefully camouflaged with aubrietia.

We longed to go down into this room, but of course the war was over and the room was being slowly filled up with garden rubbish. We loved to tip stones and weeds down the shafts from above and listen to them landing some several feet below. Mom used to dispose of all the old medicine and poison bottles down the shafts, too. I wonder what excavators of the future will think about it all.

At the side of the rockery was Dad's shed. I was not allowed inside by myself, but when I did go in with Dad, I loved everything about it. The mixed up smell of paint and wood and oil and Dad's cigarettes was powerful. He had pictures of motorbikes stuck on the walls and all manner of tools hanging up. I can remember when the bottom of the shed went rotten there was much consternation about the cost of a replacement. However, Dad and Uncle Percy dismantled the shed and built a new concrete base, plus a few courses of bricks to stand the shed on once the rotten bottom section had been cut off. They did a really good job, and when I went back to visit the house in 1997, the shed was still as good as new.

The shed afforded us much entertainment. We did handstands and played ball games up against the walls, and the long green sides were used as blackboards when we played schools. Mom still laughs about the day I was teacher and I chalked up in big letters on the side of the shed, 'How much does it cost to send a French letter to France?' Mom called the neighbours round to have a look and they were all laughing but never explained the joke to me. It was years before the penny dropped.

But the most magical thing about the shed was flying off the roof. We secretly carried an assortment of cushions from the house and tied them securely around our bottoms with string or leather belts. We used to climb (out of Mom's sight) onto the coke bunker at the back of the shed. From that position we could reach the lower slopes of the shed. Next, we would clamber on all fours up to the very apex of the roof. After surveying the world laid out before us, we crept gingerly to the very edge of the shed, stood up, stretched out our arms, flapped them wildly, held our breath, closed our eyes, and jumped. We were absolutely convinced we would be able to fly if we practised enough.

None of us ever did get the knack of flying, but we all got a lot of bumps and bangs. Mom used to be really worried and tried, in vain, to stop us – but we would yell in unison, *'What's wrong? We're only flying off the shed roof!'*

The entry was an important part of our life. The coal shed was in the entry and we had to count the sacks in when the coalman came. We got into such trouble if we lost count, as Mom only wanted to pay for what had been delivered. There were always two rather dusty-looking men, with very white eyes, carrying sacks on their backs and we got extremely confused by their comings and goings. We were more interested in studying them, their horses and cart, and their big weights and scales, than we were in counting the coal sacks.

A really vivid memory is of Mom skipping in the entry. I don't know why she only skipped there – perhaps she felt shy in front of the neighbours and couldn't be seen in this bit of the garden. I loved to see her skip and she was very good at it. She would fold up the washing line into the right length and skip and skip, singing all the old rhymes from her youth. It is this memory of her that makes me the saddest now with her deteriorating health – she used to skip so well, and now she stumbles as she walks.

The entry was an extension of the kitchen. Dad sharpened the knives on the stone back step – I shudder at the remembered scraping noise it made. For some reason we always sat on the back kitchen step to shell peas. We had a bag full of peas and the colander and had to sit there until they were done. We ate an awful lot of peas in the process, but I liked to eat the shells as well. Of course, these are sold now as the posh 'mangetout'.

I have another memory of Mom banging the wooden boards that ran along the entry between our house and the one next door. Once Mom had attracted the neighbour's attention, they would stand on their respective steps to have a good gossip over the boards. If they wanted to tell secrets they would get down off their steps, walk along the boards to a lower place and whisper, whisper…

Beyond the rockery and the shed was the most formal part of the garden; a lovely green lawn with a long flower bed between us and Mrs Cowper, and a narrower border with a chequered path on the other side, next to Mrs Harvey. At the end of the lawn there was rose trellising and in front of this was 'the bench'.

Mom and Dad had bought the bench at a house sale across the road. It had once been the most beautifully carved oak settee, upholstered in very expensive embroidered damask. There were little padded cushions on the arms, as well as cushions affixed to the back and the long seat. Dad was not a bit impressed by any of this and stripped off every bit of material, before getting out the paint can to cover the lovely old oak with several layers of green paint.

The bench was much admired by everyone who came to the house, and the whole family spent many happy years sitting on it. As the family moved from house to house, the bench moved, too. It was, indeed, a very sad day when, after Dad's death, the bench finally disintegrated and had to be scrapped. Mom kept one arm from it for ages – she simply couldn't bear to part with this memento of our family life.

Behind the rose bower were the vegetable garden and our playground. Dad and Uncle Percy managed the vegetable garden between them; it was on the left-hand side of the garden, next door to the Cowpers. Dad always believed that 'Old Cowper' chucked his stones over into our garden, as well as allowing his squitch grass to grow through into our borders.

On the right-hand side of the top garden was a much rougher lawn where we could play without getting into trouble for spoiling the grass. We also had a swing and a see-saw. Dad made the swing, and it stood up to years and years of play – there never was a stronger swing. The see-saw was made by placing the decorating plank across a sturdy wooden saw bench that had been fashioned from an old railway sleeper. We had marvellous times on that see-saw but never seemed able to get the weight balanced correctly. I can remember going down to the ground with a thump ever so many times – we probably ruined our backs for life.

The shed at the far end of our boundary was used for gardening tools. There were all sorts of things which had belonged to my paternal Grandfather, which we don't seem to have now. Dad had special names for them and would say something like, 'Fetch me the curly rake' – and it really was curly like a great, clawed hand and wonderful for raking. Outside the shed was a water butt, rusty and standing on bricks. We were forbidden to climb up to it, but of course we did because we discovered fascinating little fish swimming back and forth in there. In truth they were simply the small darting insects that appear in stagnant water everywhere, but we spent many happy hours trying to catch them in jam jars.

But the icing on the cake in the top part of the garden was our very own miniature house built by Dad for us to play in. We were so lucky; it was a beautiful house made completely from wood with little windows and a doorway. It measured about nine feet square, allowing plenty of room for four small girls, their toys and their teddies and their tea parties. We spent many long hours within its walls making meals for our dolls and our friends.

Stones became potatoes; vegetables were cabbage leaves or grass, sticks made the most wonderful lamb chops, and water from the butt mixed with a little earth made the gravy.

We had real meals in there too. I can see Mom so clearly making the long walk from the house with plates of chips for us to eat at weekends and in the school holidays.

At the end of the garden was a fence and beyond the fence were the allotments. We often used to climb the fence to walk and play over there. I loved the individual square plots with their boundaries of stones or bricks. I admired the narrow dusty paths that had been made by the constant tramping of wellington boots.

Each gardener had a shed. Some achieved a pretty doll's house effect, with neat wooden buildings complete with windows, doors and curtains. Others used obsolete Anderson air raid shelters, and still more used an odd assortment of whatever came to hand to create ramshackle shelters. All seemed to have a chair to sit on and a metal bin in which to burn rubbish. Pea and bean sticks, bundles of raffia ties, forks, shovels, rakes and hoes, water butts, wheelbarrows and compost heaps all jostled for position in the limited space available. I loved the haphazard mixture of vegetables, fruit and flowers, and I was fascinated by the many different bird scarers: waving bits of paper on sticks, silver milk bottle tops on strings, paper windmills and strangely clad scarecrows.

People seemed much more kindly then; we would wander round the allotments for hours and hours and would often be given a cabbage or a few potatoes, rhubarb or sweet peas to take home. We considered the plot holders to be our neighbours, as were all the people in our road.

There were Mr and Mrs Cowper, who gave us tins of Sharp's toffee for Christmas; Mr and Mrs Harvey, who kept their garden so neatly and had a fishpond; Mrs Williams, who sold Mom the odd tomato for our tea; Mrs Dean, who always sat with her feet up on a stool because she had suffered many miscarriages; Mr Bownds, who drove Dad mad with his infantile humour; Mrs Grigg, who had a poor little 'blue baby'; Mrs Tilley, who had four or five small children and was agoraphobic; and neighbours who were posh and showed it by having signs on their gate saying, 'No Pedlars, No Hawkers'.

We knew them all and they knew us. We looked out for one another and never had to lock our doors; it was a different world from the one I live in now.

This house, then, in Aldridge Road, together with the garden, the neighbours, and the allotments was our milieu for many years; the environment wherein we learned to fly. Were we lucky – I believe so!

High Days and Holidays

We had very little for Christmas when we were young, but even so we were extremely excited by the thought of a special present. The emphasis at school and at church was on the religious aspect of Christmas, and we treated the holiday with reverence. We had Christmas plays, carol singing and baby Jesus in his manger, and spent many hours glorifying the Lord.

As times were hard and goods in short supply, we learned to be satisfied with our lot. As the magical day approached we started working on our letters to Father Christmas; we asked for one present only – whatever was dearest to our heart at that particular time. On Christmas Eve we were allowed to put our letters up the chimney; everybody had a coal fire with a good upward draught. Mom or Dad used to remove the fireguard and hold us firmly by the back of our dresses whilst we leaned forward to let the letters fly up the chimney. We really believed that one of Father Christmas's helpers collected the messages at the top.

On Christmas Eve we put up the tree. It was always a real tree with that unmistakable pine needle smell. Dad and Uncle Percy used to get the trees from Cannock Chase. Dad would put our tree in a big galvanised bucket filled with earth before artistically decorating it with red crêpe paper tied round with a satin bow. We had really pretty, delicate glass baubles to hang on our tree that Dad had brought home from Germany. We also had streamers of silver tinsel, and a magical fairy with outstretched wings and a halo for the top. Our coloured fairy lights were unusual and of every shape and size; there were lanterns, acorns, bells, snowmen, pineapples, stars, moons and cheerful Father Christmases.

Once the tree was decorated we went up to bed with Dad's thick white wellington boot socks to hang on the bedpost. We lay awake for hours trying to spot the moment when Father Christmas came through the door with our gifts. Of course, we

99

never saw him. In the morning we would wake with great excitement and rush with our filled socks into Mom and Dad's room. I get a sad feeling now when I remember how thrilled we were with so very little, and realise how materialistic and disenchanted most children of today are.

The socks looked misshapen and knobbly and we could hardly wait to empty them. In each sock was a walnut, an orange, a hollow chocolate Father Christmas, a pencil, a tin of toffees, a cardboard game such as snakes and ladders, a home-made jigsaw, and our special present. I still have my doll that was my special present when I was six. I loved her immediately and played with her for very many years; she is battered and broken now but I love her still. Both my daughter and granddaughter have played with her, and she has had trips to two schools to teach modern-day children about the toys of yesteryear. I called her 'June April' initially, but eventually changed her name to Julie.

I remember one particular year when Dad made each of us a kaleidoscope. They were magical and he must have struggled to make four of them. Somehow he had managed to obtain the mirrored glass, the eyepieces, the glass bases and the little coloured beads to put inside. They were a complicated design and must have tried his patience to the limit. I wish I still had mine today; I don't know what happened to it, and hope I was not careless with something he tried so hard to please me with.

Mom and Dad had very few gifts themselves; I think maybe they got each other a couple of presents to keep the magic of Christmas alive for us children. I do remember that Dad was very aggravating about opening presents. He simply would not open them quickly. Most presents were wrapped with pretty paper and string that had already been used a dozen times, but Dad was adamant things had to be opened carefully so that the paper could be used yet again. He would slowly undo the knots in the string and carefully roll it into a ball; next he would unwrap the paper and smooth and fold it neatly; finally he would examine his present and say, 'Ah, very nice. That's all right. That'll do,' before putting it down at the side of the bed.

Eventually we trundled downstairs for breakfast. It used to be slightly more extravagant than usual, and we had a little bit of bacon and mushroom instead of our normal Weetabix. Mom was always very busy on Christmas Day because we often had a large gathering for dinner and tea, and she had to get the turkey cooked – with all the trimmings. Poultry didn't come oven-ready from the butcher or supermarket; it came complete with its head dangling down on a long neck, its feathers and, worst of all, its bloody innards.

Uncle Percy used to come from Lichfield on Christmas Eve to 'dress' the bird. Firstly, he undertook the extremely time-consuming task of plucking out the feathers. Some were tough and wouldn't come out completely, leaving sharp stubby quills behind. The quills had to be burned off with a match. Some folks kept the feathers and put them inside sacks of material called ticking and used them for pillows. Next, Uncle Percy put layers and layers of newspaper on the kitchen table where the poor old bird would be plonked unceremoniously down. Without further ado, Uncle Percy sharpened the big kitchen knife on the steel, and – off with its head! Following this, he would put his hand inside the bird and pull out all sorts of unpleasant things; some were truly horrid and were thrown away, but others, such as the heart, kidneys and neck, were put in a saucepan and used to make stock or gravy. There was one part of the anatomy called a 'craw' that had to be handled very carefully; if it burst it could cause the turkey to taste very bitter.

Once the turkey had been thoroughly washed inside and out it was handed over to Mom for the cooking. The turkey's body was filled with home-made thyme and parsley stuffing, and the breast covered with strips of streaky bacon before being cooked for many long hours in the oven.

To accompany the turkey we had roast potatoes, mashed potatoes, sprouts, peas, carrots, stuffing balls and sausage, all covered generously with thick, rich gravy.

Dinner time on Christmas Day was never before two o'clock. The table was set with the best cloth and lots of mats for the hot dishes. Mom had a good array of decent cutlery and it was all used on this special day. Ordinary people didn't have wine in those days, but I seem to remember we children were allowed to have pop, and the grown-ups had sherry.

When the turkey was ready it was brought, with great ceremony, to the table for carving. It was always the man of the household who carved and, in our house at least, it was always Dad who tasted the first bit of meat. We would sit around the table with our salivary glands working nineteen to the dozen whilst Dad sliced enough meat for each plate. Each person had a little bit of breast meat and a little bit off the leg or underside of the bird. There was always a squabble over the parson's nose and the wishbone! It was a free-for-all to get your vegetables before everything went cold. Mom was always the last to sit down, since she tried to mastermind everything in the kitchen as well as look after the many visitors and children.

Once the dinner plates had been removed, we would wait with great excitement for the pudding to be brought in. Sometimes it was a long wait because Mom still had to make the custard. This took quite a while, because the entire range of saucepans, plates and jugs had already been used to produce the first course, and needed to be washed and dried before they could be used again.

When the custard eventually came in Dad would pour brandy over the pudding and light it with his cigarette lighter. We got so excited when the flames shot up into the air and all blew furiously to 'dowt' them before the pudding got too burned. We each had a small portion of pudding and custard and, if we had room, a mince pie as well. We had to eat our pudding very carefully because, as tradition decreed, silver sixpences were put in the puddings for luck. After the pudding, we always had a few extra goodies for the table. There would be an assortment of walnuts, Brazil nuts, hazelnuts, monkey nuts, dates, tangerines and crystallised slices of lemon and orange with a sugary coating.

After dinner everyone would sit quiet and still and listen to the King's speech on the radio (later the Queen's). It was a really important part of the day, and absolutely everybody all over the country came to a standstill for it. We didn't dare make a peep for the fifteen or so minutes that it took for the King to speak to the nation. The theme of the King's speech was headline news and a major talking point for many days. We really did honour the Royal Family, and I think they were probably deserving of our respect then; now, sadly, they seem to be an anachronism.

Once the King's speech was over, we scattered in our different directions. Moms and aunties went to the kitchen to tackle the mountain of washing up; dads and uncles either talked or fell asleep in the armchairs; and the children went hither and thither playing with their new games and toys.

We always had a lovely tea on Christmas Day, too. Tea was not served until quite late – probably seven or eight o'clock. Of course, there was cold turkey for sandwiches, as well as leftover stuffing and sausage. We had all sorts of pickles to eat with the cold meat, such as Spanish onion in vinegar, bright yellow piccalilli or red cabbage. Mom always made a nice trifle and some rock cakes too. We had the leftover mince pies and, of course, a Christmas cake.

Mom used to make really good fruit cake, but she left the icing to Dad. He had a lovely old metal icing set and he used to cover the cake with beautiful iced stars, usually bright pink in colour. We always had a snowman, a robin and a couple of little fir trees to stick on the top, and the whole thing would be encircled in a frill of red and gold. After our unusually large dinner, nobody could eat much tea except for Lorna. She was as thin as a lath when she was a little girl, but she could eat and eat we used to tease her that she had a tapeworm. Lorna never felt she had had a truly happy Christmas unless she was sick on Christmas night and, to be honest, we looked forward to her being sick too, because it came to be one of our family traditions.

After tea everyone would join in with the games. There are four that really stick in my mind, and we played them year in and year out: the Moon is Round, Jumping from an Aeroplane, Having a Baby, and Following the Light.

For the Moon is Round, we had to sit in a circle and draw a moon-face on the floor. The 'hidden' rule was to move the pencil from your right to your left hand before passing the pencil to the next person. You couldn't win unless you remembered to do this. It occurs to me now that there was no allowance made in this game for naturally left-handed people. Of course, when I was growing up no one was allowed to use his or her left hand either at home or at school.

Jumping from an Aeroplane was great fun. A blindfolded child had to jump from a wobbling plank (the aeroplane), as it was about to crash. The 'plane' seemed to be near the ceiling but, in fact, it was only inches from the ground. We were often scared to jump.

Having a Baby was rather a weird game. A little bit of lipstick and a tea towel turned your hand and arm into a swaddled baby after a blindfolded visit to 'hospital'. Some of the 'babies' our parents created were rather ugly.

For Following the Light we had to follow a round circle of light by pressing our nose up against a white sheet behind which Dad held the torch.

Dad used to weave very complicated journeys up and down and round the sheet, but eventually would lead us – by the nose – to the very top of the sheet, where he dabbed us liberally in the face with his soapy shaving brush.

These were such simple, homespun games, but we loved them all. We played them over and over again and it just didn't seem to matter that we knew exactly what was coming. Of course, Christmas was a great time, too, for playing the piano, having a sing-song and getting Uncle Fred to give us a few tunes on the 'spoons'. We all tried to do the Charleston and the Black Bottom and there was always much joy and laughter.

Our next festival was Easter. There were many extra church services at this time of year, as well as sermons about making sacrifices for Lent. We rarely gave up anything in the food department, as we all felt half starved anyway. In church on Palm Sunday we were given a palm leaf in the shape of a cross, which we brought home and used as a bookmark in our Bibles.

We looked forward enormously to having pancakes and hot cross buns. When I was a child, these treats appeared only at Easter – we didn't see them again for a whole year. Mom used to make us two pancakes each; all that could be managed from our meagre post-war rations. Usually we had a small amount of sugar and lemon juice on our pancakes or, if we were lucky, a dollop of treacle dropped from a great height off a spoon so that it ran in the thinnest possible drizzle over the surface of the pancake.

Mom tried her best to toss the pancakes but was rarely successful. They usually landed half in and half out of the frying pan. If they hit the floor they were wiped clean and eaten just the same. We loved to fold the pancakes over and over and there was fierce competition to see who could make the most rolls out of their pancake.

Hot cross buns were ordered specially from the baker. Those today are a very poor imitation of the ones we used to get. They were really fresh, baked that very morning, with a lovely cross on the top and smelling of spices and fruit. We didn't have any butter to put on them, but they were an enormous treat even so. We had one bun each.

When rationing relaxed and ingredients became a little more easily available, Mom and all my aunts began making traditional simnel cakes again. They were lovely, with a layer of toasted marzipan on the top. Small pieces of leftover marzipan were fashioned into egg-shaped pieces and placed in a circle round the top of the cake. A fluffy, bright yellow chicken with an orange beak sat in the middle. I don't know how or why simnel cakes came to be traditional at Easter. On checking in the *Oxford Dictionary*, I find the definition for simnel is: 'a rich ornamental cake baked especially at Easter, often with a marzipan layer or decoration'.

We didn't get chocolate Easter eggs until I reached my teenage years because of rationing. Chocolate began to appear fairly freely again in about 1954, when I was twelve. So for many years we had hard-boiled hens' eggs at Easter, which we decorated with our paints. Linda, Lorna and Jennifer ate theirs on Easter Sunday morning, but I couldn't eat mine because of my allergy to eggs. So Easter, really, was a non-event for me.

One year Dad decided to get each of us a set of compasses, coloured pencils, paper and rubbers for our Easter gifts. I expect it seems a boring present today, so it is difficult to describe how thrilled we were and how many happy hours we spent round the dining table drawing and colouring the most fantastic patterns. The patterns got bigger and bigger and more and more intricate and it soon became a craze at school – everyone wanted a compass. We rarely used our compasses for their intended purpose of drawing circles and understanding circumference. And for once I could join in with the others with an Easter gift, which gave me great pleasure.

We didn't often go for a 'day out' on Easter Monday as most people did. Mom and Dad thought everywhere was too busy; they preferred to save their petrol ration for quieter times, rather than wasting it sitting in a traffic jam. The weather at Easter was usually bitterly cold, and there was often snow. Sometimes, Easter is celebrated in early March; as I write today (2003), Easter Sunday falls on 20 April. The later date, together with climate changes, has meant a change for the better for the holiday weather. I find it amazing that the date of a major Christian festival should be moveable, and sometimes have snow, and sometimes have warm sunshine!

As the year slipped round into summer, we became excited at the prospect of days out and holidays at the seaside. We were luckier than many children of my generation; most never went further from home than the Lickey Hills, Barr Beacon or Sutton Park. We enjoyed the local beauty spots, too, but Dad had travelled widely with the Air Force and with his work for British Timken, and was determined that 'his girls' should see as much of the world as possible, as soon as possible.

When we were small, and before Jennifer was born, our mode of transport was a lovely little Austin Seven. Mostly, we went to places in Wales such as Lake Vyrnwy, Fairbourne, Dolgoch Falls, the Horseshoe Pass, Betws-y-Coed and Snowdonia. Our dear little car struggled valiantly up extremely steep hills such as Dinas Mawddwy. Nearly all the cars had to stop halfway because they were boiling up. Special stopping places had been cut out of the side of the steep 1 in 3 gradient for cars to cool down before adding more water to the radiator. On the return journey the downward hill was so steep that cutting out places had been made for cars to 'bank it' should they suffer failure from overheated brakes.

The Austin had a sunshine roof, which Dad opened so that Linda and I could stand on the hump of the transmission shaft to stick our heads out of the roof. There were no worries about seat belts – there wasn't the volume of traffic or the speed of modern day cars to concern us. The Austin had a winding handle on the dash that was used to open up the windscreen to improve visibility if there was fog or torrential rain. The car had only one central windscreen wiper, which went very slowly backwards and forwards. The trafficators were quaint orange triangles on a lever mechanism. When a switch was flicked on the dashboard the appropriate triangle popped out from the top of the door pillar to indicate a turn.

We had two doors on our car, whereas some had four, but the rear doors on some cars were dangerous and were called 'suicide doors'. Instead of opening forwards as on modern cars, the doors opened backwards, and if a small child in the rear seat fidgeted and fell on the door handle, the door flew open leaving a gaping chasm for the child to fall out. There were no child seats, seat belts, central locking systems or safety catches.

Cousin Roger had such an accident when we were on an outing in Uncle Bill's taxi. He had a nasty fall from the car whilst travelling at high speed and bears scars on his face as a result. I seem to remember he broke his arm at the same time.

Sometimes, for our summer holiday, we travelled to Devon or Cornwall. Occasionally we stayed in a caravan and shared our holiday with Aunty Lil, Uncle Percy and Pamela to keep the costs down. At other times, we went camping with Dad's ancient and patched khaki army tent and rickety Primus stove. We treated the Primus stove with great respect, but even so Dad occasionally set the tent on fire by brewing up too close to the canvas.

Once, however, we stayed in what were commonly known in those days as 'digs'. I think it was probably very cheap dinner, bed and breakfast accommodation. When I look back now at how poorly off we were I don't know how Mom and Dad afforded even that. There must have been some very careful saving done. I am sure they thought it a great treat, and it must have been wonderful for Mom to have a proper holiday with her meals cooked for her every day. But, oh dear, the food was awful! Day after day for a whole week, every meal consisted of marrow in every shape and form – boiled, mashed, roast, cubed, and stuffed. It was bright yellow in colour, of a watery consistency, with no taste whatsoever. I am sure marrow can probably taste quite nice, but I think because I sat, heaving and heaving, in front of so many plates of the hideous stuff, I don't have the stomach for it now.

And one year, we went to Burnham-on-Sea, perhaps because of its proximity to Bridgwater Bay. I have put off writing this chapter because of a terrifying experience on this holiday. Nightmares continue to this day. Mom and Dad had hired a caravan for a week or a fortnight, and off we went in great excitement for our time at the seaside.

I was about nine, Linda ten, Lorna seven and Jen just a toddler of two. We loved spending our days on the beach and having a walk, chasing the waves, at night.

Because I have deliberately shut out memories of this holiday, the details are sketchy. I remember we were having an early evening walk along the beach; Mom and us girls were near the water's edge, and Dad was lingering much further back talking to a group of people with beached boats. Suddenly, without any warning whatsoever, a gigantic wave leaped at us from nowhere, covering us completely with ice-cold water before rushing us out to sea. Linda could swim a little, but even so she was bashed unmercifully against the rocks. Lorna and I were simply swept beneath the cold and frightening water with enormous force. I was terrified, my lungs felt full of water, and although I am sure I struggled furiously I could not break free of the waves or raise my head above the water. Lorna was in the same danger as me. I must have risen above the water for a moment though because I have a very clear picture in my head of Mom, far out at sea, holding Jennifer above her head.

Dad ran crazily up and down the beach, not knowing what to do or who to try to save first. Luckily, there were people with boats on the beach, and I am told rope was gathered up and people braved the torrential waters to save us.

The sea was far too rough and dangerous for the boats to be launched, but the equipment they carried saved our lives. I make no secret of the fact that I hate the water, especially the sea; I have never learned to swim and feel sick when I am near water. All my nightmares are about drowning or about those I love drowning. The episode has marred my life and I have great respect for the power of the sea. Despite my terror I have been determined that my children should learn to swim well at an early age, and am relieved that my grandchildren, too, can swim and love the sea.

Over the years I have heard of many similar tragedies. The sea at Burnham has a very fast rising high tide, with twin currents. There are also dangerous quicksands in the area. Today there are very sketchy notices about the risks; there were none when we experienced the treachery of the sea in 1951. In 2002 I relived my nightmares on hearing of the death of a five-year-old child who became trapped by the quicksand and was covered by the sea. No one could get near enough to save her, and I cried and cried to imagine the terror of her slow death as she was sucked down and the grief of her parents as they looked helplessly on.

As we grew older, and things became easier, Dad decided to take us abroad to Belgium, France, Germany, Austria, Switzerland, Italy and Venice for a grand tour. This was unheard of in the 1950s for ordinary families like ours – and we were much envied at school.

The first time we went, I think Dad still had his old Triumph (AWD 861), but on subsequent visits we went in the 'Beetle'. Dad was one of the first people in England to have a Volkswagen Beetle, and belonged to the original owners' club. It sounds unsophisticated now, but in those days Beetle owners gave each other a salute as they passed on the road. Many British people thought it was dreadful to have a German car so soon after the war and said so. Other people were amazed to see that the engine of the car was at the back, and that the luggage was stored under the bonnet.

We were so excited the first time we arrived in Dover and realised we were going to cross the Channel on a boat. It was a lovely experience visiting foreign countries, and everywhere we went people were wonderfully friendly and fascinated by 'the four little English sisters'.

We saw the Black Forest, the Grossglockner Pass, the Heidelberg film set of *The Student Prince*, the Italian lakes, the Eiffel Tower, the Arc de Triomphe, the Rialto Bridge, the Doge's Palace, the many pinnacled schlosses in Germany, and the Dolomite Mountains.

We travelled on the autobahns and the autostrade – our first experience of motorways. We saw fairy-tale Swiss cottages with cows stabled beneath the houses, and cows with bells around their necks that clanged as they walked. We saw roadside shrines and magnificent cake shops with choux pastry swans; we tasted spaghetti for the first time, Wurze sauce and Wiener schnitzel.

We slept with duck-feather filled duvets on our beds and marvelled at how they were hung out of the windows to air, we heard the clamour of church bells in every Italian village, we fed the pigeons in St Mark's Square and were amazed by the marvel of Venice; we collected clouds in a matchbox at the top of the Stelvio Pass, and edelweiss from the slopes of an Austrian mountain.

We were amazed to see that the French police had real guns and that the Italian traffic police stood on boxes in the middle of the road; we admired the daring of young boys as they stood on running boards to direct motorists through busy traffic for a few lire pocket money; we bought beautiful silk badges everywhere we visited and had our passport stamped at many different checkpoints as we crossed the borders from Belgium to Holland to Switzerland to France to Germany to Italy, and so on.

We watched whole families of Italians sitting on the pavement in the late evening sun around a small television set; we saw wedding processions in the street in Salzburg and grown men in leather shorts with briefcases going to work in Germany.

The new experiences were endless and breathtaking and we learned so much, by osmosis, as you do when you are young. We were incredibly lucky children with very far-seeing parents. Travel is always exciting, and I still get that breathless feeling experienced as a child when I get in a car to start a journey... and I still get homesick after a while and feel a need to return to my roots. My favourite homecoming sight now, as it was then, is the appearance of the white cliffs of Dover as the ferry returns from France.

The summer gave way to autumn, and in November we celebrated Bonfire Night. We made no festival of Halloween, as youngsters do today; it has been imported quite recently from America, and seems to include a growing custom with youngsters here that is popularly called 'trick or treat'.

But Bonfire Night was another matter, and we loved it. For weeks and weeks children collected orange boxes from the greengrocers, old tree stumps and branches, surplus furniture, tyres and settees. We didn't worry about air pollution or the acrid black smoke that came from the horsehair sofas and rubber tyres. We always had a guy for the top of the fire that was made from old jumpers and trousers stuffed with newspapers or straw. We would try to find a chair to sit the guy on so that he could look down on us from his lofty perch as the flames leaped around him.

We had lovely Bonfire Night food, too. We had potatoes and chestnuts cooked in the hot ashes of the fire. They were burned black on the skins and we had no butter or salt to go with them, but they tasted delicious. We had white and blue enamelled mugs full of milky cocoa to wash it all down. Dad had woven string neatly round and round the handles of the mugs to prevent them from burning our hands. He called it 'whipcording'.

Bonfire Night was always bitterly cold and we wore a lot of clothes – hats and coats, and jumpers, and scarves, and mittens and wellington boots with thick grey woollen socks held up by elastic garters. We stood as near to the fire as we were allowed in order to keep warm, and stamped our feet on the hard frozen earth to improve the circulation in our numb toes.

Dad was usually in charge at our family bonfires when all the aunts, uncles and cousins gathered together for the evening. He set the fireworks off at a safe distance from the crowd and was brilliant at pinning Catherine wheels to a fence post so that they whizzed round and round at terrific speed without sticking and spoiling the display. He used old milk bottles to launch the rockets, which shot into the air at a wonderful speed shooting stars to left and right. We had jumping jacks and Golden Rain and many more whose names I can't remember. Best of all we loved the sparklers, because we were allowed to hold them in our hands. We loved to wave them about making magical patterns and whirligigs in the air. We were also allowed to hold Bengal matches that burst into coloured flames of red, or yellow or green, with a satisfying hiss.

At the end of the evening we were all tucked up in bed together whilst the grown-ups continued the party until the early hours. We went to bed with dirty faces and smelling wonderfully of smoke, to dream the night away. Next morning was nearly as exciting as we went out to explore the remains of the bonfire, to poke the ashes with sticks and to examine the burnt-out fireworks. We would hold on to the spent rockets with their sharp wooden sticks for days and days. I am sure each generation becomes more and more sophisticated, but we loved the simple pleasure of standing in the dark, eating burned food and holding our sparklers.

And so the year moved round once more to Christmas, and it all began again. But interspersed with the religious festivals and summer holidays were our birthdays, and for many years we all had tea parties. Linda's party was in February, Jennifer's in March, mine in September and Lorna's in December, so the year was neatly punctuated by numerous celebrations.

Birthday tea parties, when we were young, were very simple. We were allowed to invite four or five friends from school and, together with sisters and cousins, we made a party of twelve or so. Guests didn't normally bring presents; it simply wasn't expected – or possible.

I am sure we wore our best frocks and socks and had fresh ribbons for our hair, but I really don't remember. The thing most looked forward to, and that which caused the greatest excitement, was 'the tea'. Because our daily diet was so meagre, tasteless and boring, we longed passionately for a change. Birthday teas provided that change and helped us to endure the weeks in between. Mothers must have struggled incessantly to salt away 'goodies' for special days. Today's youngsters would sneer at their efforts, but believe me, their skilfulness brightened our days beyond imagination.

The tea began with either salmon paste or potted beef sandwiches, cut into tiny triangles, with a bit of cress or a slice of tomato as an accompaniment. Crisps didn't exist in our world. The sandwiches were made from white bread. Dad reckoned brown bread was made from the dirty sweepings from the floor at the end of the day once all the white bread had been made – and he wouldn't have it in the house!

After the sandwiches, we had peaches and cream (Carnation

evaporated milk) with half a slice of bread and butter to mop up the juice. Next, we had strawberry jelly in the shape of a rabbit with a slice of Lyons ice cream on top. The ice cream came wrapped in paper, and you had to peel the paper off your slice before you could eat it. We all enjoyed licking the paper. We had tiny iced biscuits called Little Gems, and fairy cakes with a blob of pink icing and a sprinkling of hundreds and thousands on the top. And to drink we had a rare treat – a sweet and fizzy red pop called ice cream soda.

And, of course, we had birthday cake – a sponge cake made by Mom and iced by Dad, with the appropriate number of candles to be blown out and wished upon. Cake wasn't eaten at the party, but wrapped in greaseproof paper and put by the coats and hats to be taken home to share with the family. There was no such thing as a goody bag.

After tea we played games: blind man's buff, pin the tail on the donkey, oranges and lemons, musical chairs, pass the parcel and Lucy Lockett. Children nowadays have the most fantastic and expensive parties at the Wacky Warehouse or McDonald's, or Children's Farm, or ice skating, or swimming – the list is endless.

I am pleased to say that my grandchildren have mostly had fairly simple birthday tea parties at home, with the old games and the unsophisticated food that we enjoyed. I have a sneaky feeling that all their little guests have thoroughly enjoyed the novelty of being invited to a homespun party, and that they have enjoyed playing those same games that have endured since Victorian times and before.

I can't say that my childhood was unhappy, but my sisters and I did grow up in very austere times. Large parts of our young lives were spent without our father or, indeed, any adult males. This made the festivals of the year – our high days and holidays – doubly valuable.

It seems strange that, as times have become easier and people are better off, many families are split asunder. When I was in my early twenties and feeling drained physically, financially and emotionally by my four toddlers, Dad said to me that when you stopped struggling you stopped loving. I think he was right. I do place much greater value on those things that have been hard won; I am not too impressed with the immediate satisfaction of an instant 'shop-bought' style of living.

When I look back, I marvel at how my parents and my aunts and uncles managed, and I am full of admiration for their determination to hold the family together through troubled times. The glue was good, and by sharing celebrations with one another it was possible to overcome the hardships of war, rationing and poverty. We came through it all and, hopefully, have been able to pass on the stoicism, as well as the family traditions, to our children.

Postscript

I am conscious that I have touched briefly on the lives of my many cousins in their grown-up years. I have not, however, brought the reader up to date with my own life and that of Linda, Lorna and Jennifer – 'the four little English sisters'.

Linda is sixty-seven. She neither married nor had children, but has been living with a partner for the past sixteen years. Linda worked in Birmingham and Bournemouth for thirty-five years for Mr 'Teasey Weasey' Raymond under the professional name of 'Lucille'. Linda was hairdresser to many stars of stage, screen and television, including Michelle Dotrice, Anita Harris, Noele Gordon, Beryl Reid, Jean Morton, Jan Leeming – and many, many more. Linda is now retired and lives in Staffordshire.

Lorna is sixty-three and lives in London. She was recently widowed after almost forty years of marriage. She has a son and a daughter and one granddaughter. Lorna trained as a nurse at Good Hope Hospital, Sutton Coldfield, University College Hospital, London and Addenbrooke's Hospital, Cambridge. She and her husband lived and worked in Germany for two years in the early seventies. Lorna retired recently finishing her lifelong career in the Health Service as Lecturer in evidence-based care and management of clinical risk.

Jennifer is fifty-nine and lives in South Birmingham. She was married for eleven years, divorced, and subsequently lived with a partner for eleven years; she has no children. On leaving school, Jennifer trained as a Nursery Nurse at Garrison Lane, Birmingham; worked as an NNEB at Canterbury Cross, Perry Barr, and then trained as a teacher at West Midlands College of Education. She retired in 2004 after thirty-two years of teaching Drama, PE, Art, Modern Foreign Languages and English in Staffordshire, Hereford and Worcester Schools. Jennifer now travels the world, and has a second home in Portugal.

I am sixty-five. I was married when I was twenty to a divorcee who already had one son. We were married for twenty years and had three sons and a daughter. After my divorce, I met my current partner (who also had one son) and we have been together for twenty-six years.

Three of my six children and stepchildren have died, unnaturally, during the past eighteen years: Matthew in 1990, Scott in 1995 and Steven in 2008. Their early deaths have, in part, been my motivation for setting down memories of my early life. Much can be lost to future generations in the most unexpected ways.

Most of my professional working life has been 'people-centred'. On leaving school I worked in the Central Personnel Division of the Dunlop Rubber Company (Fort Dunlop) before taking a break to raise my family.

From the mid-eighties onward I worked firstly with NCH Action for Children, and subsequently with Home-Start Sutton Coldfield until my retirement in 2005.

I now live in a village in Staffordshire where I while away my days, writing, gardening and welcoming my family, including five fascinating grandchildren whom, hopefully…

…*I'm teaching to fly*, but not necessarily *off the shed roof!*